Tishi

Tishi

REFUGEE • IMMIGRANT • MOTHER

ANNELIESE TICHI HUNT

with Leslie Scarborough

Photo: Anneliese and friend circa 1944,
outside Misslitz (Anneliese is on the right)

Tishi
REFUGEE • IMMIGRANT • MOTHER

First Edition
Copyright ©2017 by Leslie Scarborough

All rights reserved. Without limiting the rights under copyright reserved above, no part of this publication may be reproduced, stored in or introduced into a retrieval system, or transmitted, in any form, or by any means (electronic, mechanical, photocopying, recording, or otherwise) without prior written permission of the copyright owner.

All photos from the personal Hunt family collection.

Designed by Steven Averill

ISBN-13: 978-1-948543-33-0
ISBN-10: 1-948543-33-8

Cover Photo: Tishi in New York Harbor, one day after arriving in the United States. September, 1957

*Special Thanks to
Susan Hunt*

Thanks for the encouragement, support, inspiration and/or guidance:

Jeanie Barnett, Dashel Scarborough, Hunter Scarborough, Karleen Hunt Basch, Andrew Basch, Mark and Robin Hunt, and of course, my dad, William Lynn Hunt, Heather Hansen, Pamela Martin, David Catrambone, Jane Kellard, Steven Averill, Cindy Landon, Lisa London, Kit Rice Landi, Bob Brengle, Jesse Vint III, Gary Markowitz, June Pierce, Dane Scarborough, Dr. David Vesco, Lacy Williams, and our darling Kirstin Hunt.

Table of Contents

Introduction by Leslie Scarborough 1

Chapter 1 – **Czechoslovakia 1934-1945** 5

Chapter 2 – **The Russians and The Czechs** 11

Chapter 3 – **Becoming a Refugee** 17

Chapter 4 – **Rebuilding: In and Around Ulm 1946-1949** 23

Chapter 5 – **Moving into the Fifties: Of Boys and Men** 31

Chapter 6 – **The Winds of Change** 47

Chapter 7 – **Love, Marriage and America** 57

Chapter 8 – **Heartbreak** 69

Chapter 9 – **Picking Up and Going On** 71

Chapter 10 – **Ithaca, New York** 79

Chapter 11 – **Chicago 1966-1976** 87

Epilogue 2017 107

Addendum – A Daughters Reaction and Recollections............111

Conclusion 129

Introduction

By Leslie Scarborough

American novelist Elmore Leonard gave this classic advice to writers: "When you write, try to leave out all the parts readers will skip." Introductions are notoriously skipped, so I will make this brief, and I ask you to hang in there with me.

I am Leslie Scarborough, eldest daughter of Anneliese Tichi Hunt. My mother was a German child during World War II, and a refugee in post-Nazi Germany. She met my dad long after the war in the late 1950's. They were married in Germany. She moved with him to the United States, where she later became a naturalized citizen, which she was extremely proud of. Since Americans could not pronounce her first name properly (It's Ah-neh-LEEZ-eh), she went by Tishi, the Americanization of her maiden name, and the name my father called her. She believed it suited her. However, she abhorred it when people dropped the "i", and just called her "Tish". That's where she drew the line and corrected them. I just called her Mommy.

This book exists because my mother was having trouble sleeping after I went away to college in her early 40's. One doctor, after learning of her tumultuous early life, thought that maybe, with her firstborn being away, she had time to reflect. He felt that she might subconsciously be haunted by the darker events of her past. He suggested that she write down the story of her life, like a memoir. He thought it could be cathartic and freeing. My mom took the task to heart, and the outcome is in the following pages.

Tishi   REFUGEE • IMMIGRANT • MOTHER

I vaguely knew of my mom's memoir. After she died, my dad never mentioned it. He remarried a few years after her death, and when he passed away a couple of years ago, my stepmother handed me a stack of yellowed notebook paper, saying I should have it. My mom wrote it by hand, in her old German script, which means that even though it's in English, it is barely legible to Americans. My younger brother and sister were at a loss to decipher the writing, and I promised to type it up for them so they could read about our mom's life. Being the eldest, I was the one most exposed to the German language and lettering. I have no trouble reading my mother's handwriting.

As I started to transcribe her story, I realized how much I didn't know about her younger life. As I read on, so much more of a picture emerged, that it became clear what a gift she left us. At first I just thought it was a gift for our family. Although she wrote it all from the vantage point of her 40's (in the mid 1970's), she remembered so many details that filled out our family history and even the world history I thought I knew. This went far beyond her musings about the steam and aroma of hot chestnuts that vendors sold on street corners around Christmastime in Germany.

This is a walk through my mom's whole life, through her eyes. During the process of transcribing her manuscript, I would lay in bed, thinking about where I had left off in her story. I wanted to get back to my computer and her writing, and make sure she got through certain situations safely. I wanted to finish, so I could share it with my siblings. There were references to historical events that I realized they would not know about. I educated myself so I could explain them in more detail. I tried to honor her writing voice at whatever point she was at, as I did so. It dawned on me that this is a unique view from a German child, in a different European country, of a war we are used to experiencing from an American, English, French, Polish or Jewish perspective.

Following my mother's life is an historical journey. I decided this was a journey to be shared with a much larger audience.

I have deliberated whether or not she would approve of me making her life public. My mother was quite outspoken and always encouraged me to follow my heart. She wanted me to read "The Diary of

INTRODUCTION | By Leslie Scarborough

Anne Frank" long before eighth grade, when we covered it in school. It was also important to her that I read a book called "Mischling, Second Degree", a German woman's view of her experience during World War II as a child who was one quarter Jewish. I remember my mom being fascinated with the changing political landscapes of Europe and the United States. Now I have before me the documented life of a European born, American wife in the 60's and 70's, as well as a childhood story from the war, as she remembered it. My assessment is that it is exactly the kind of thing she would find intriguing. Would she have a dilemma regarding her privacy?

My heart can hear my mom answering this question in her typical fashion:

"Over my dead body. Really, if I'm dead, what does it matter?"

So here is Mommy's story:

Tishi   REFUGEE • IMMIGRANT • MOTHER

Chapter 1
Czechoslovakia 1934-1945

I was born in Brünn, Czechoslovakia July 23, 1934. My name was Anneliese Tichi. My parents were of German nationality but of Czech citizenship at the time. We lived in one of the German portions of Czechoslovakia, all of which were called the Sudetenland. Until April of 1938, I enjoyed the life of a single child; pampered, adored and catered to. I was supposedly very pretty, bright and charming, the pride and joy of my parents. My dad was a prominent dentist and my mom was what was then considered an "accomplished housewife". We were from a good family, the relatives of which also lived with and around us. We were good people.

In April, 1938, my sister Inge arrived, the new addition to our family. She was underweight and sickly. She could not tolerate my mother's milk, nor any of the different kinds of formulas available at the time. With rigorous attention and force-feeding by my parents, she survived, miraculously, although she always remained underweight and ill. Naturally, she became the focal point in our family, the main concern of my parents. I felt knocked off my pedestal in the process, and developed a hostile attitude towards her. Apparently, I kicked her baby bed and her baby buggy when she would finally be sound asleep, waking her up crying. This was not a well received gesture for the exhausted parents of a sickly, colicky child. As this happened on more than one occasion, I was punished first with a spanking, then by being put in a room for hours by myself. I was resentful for years, that no one took the trouble to explain my sister's situation to a frustrated four year old, possibly appealing to my better self. I now understand that they were simply overwhelmed and exasperated.

Later in 1938, sensing the takeover of the border areas of Czechoslovakia by Hitler, my parents moved to a town called Misslitz, which was very close to the Austrian border, and my father's childhood hometown. Since World War I, borders had been changing, and my family, as German speaking people, preferred to remain among other German speaking people and not get lumped totally into Czech culture, as they expected would happen. They did not foresee Hitler taking over all of Czechoslovakia as it actually did happen, for awhile.

The Germans in the border areas of Czechoslovakia were originally second class citizens when the country of Czechoslovakia was formed after the first World War. The German Empire, at one point, consisted of Moravia, Bohemia and Austria-Hungary. My German speaking family was there, in what had been Austria, but with the new borders drawn, they found themselves living in a foreign country, yet it was what they knew as home for generations. My grandfather fought for the rights of the German minority in the border areas by organizing all the German speaking citizens in his area and establishing himself as their leader.

Through his efforts they attained the right to vote, as well as other privileges which had been accorded to Czechs only. I believe it was in 1928 that the Germans gained representation in the Prague Parliament and my grandfather was elected Senator. He was my father's father and also later became the mayor of Misslitz, a town inhabited by Germans, Austrians, German Jews and Czechs. He was mayor of that small town until Hitler's troops marched in. Hitler had signed the Munich Agreement, which made us part of Germany again, and our family became of German citizenry once more. This was a time, one might recall, when Hitler was named "Man of the Year" by TIME magazine. He was credited with the autobahn, the Volkswagen, reducing unemployment, and lifting Germany out of its economic slump. However, not far behind, the sinister aspect of this new regime was lurking.

My grandfather welcomed the Nazi troops to Misslitz in 1938, on a

Chapter 1 | Czechoslovakia 1934-1945

tribune erected in the town square, greeting them with the Hitler salute. This attempt at placating the troops wasn't received well. He was subsequently deposed by the Nazi's for not having been German enough. They found him to be too even handed with the non-German factions in our town, and the "German" Germans stepped in. My grandfather had to prove himself worthy of even holding a job at all, so he joined the Nazi party as a paying member, just in order to be allowed to take a job as the manager of a candy factory. Not really being a fan of Hitler, but unaware of the unspeakable things that would later be carried out in his name, my grandfather stepped down from all politics, detaching himself from Hitler throughout the rest of the war period.

When our little family had moved to Misslitz in 1938, it was during the summertime, which was a good time of the year for my father to establish himself in his own dental office. In Brünn, he had been in joint practice with two other dentists. In Misslitz, his individual practice flourished in the warm summer months, and that news brought more of our family to the area before winter. My little sister continued to be sickly and underweight and seemed to me, to still be the main concern of everyone in the family. My father, mother, various relatives, and our maid, all fluttered around her. My father however, was the only one who made a concerted effort to spend time with me also. He took me on outings and played games with me. But my time with him ended abruptly in 1940 when he was drafted, and between 1940 and 1945 we saw him maybe three times for short periods only. Throughout the war he was stationed in France as part of the German occupation force. He was in the German Air Force but was not a pilot. He spent the war years before the allied invasion working at a radar station. When the allies came in, he withdrew with the German troops. We later learned he was captured by the Americans and was a prisoner of war, not tortured, but not treated very well either. He was starved to the point of eating dirt.

The early war years were uneventful in my life. Aside from missing my father, my only concerns were that I felt my friends and cousins always managed to put me in subordinate roles in our games. I still had fun playing with them, but had a recurring feeling of being thwarted. It could have simply been a projection of the bigger picture going on in my life, which was that there was a world war going on around us, but I was unaware that my irritations might have been partially due to that fact.

I loved my grandmother, who liked to stuff her grandchildren with all kinds of sweets and food. As a matter of fact, I turned to food for comfort, and became quite chubby. My mother was thrilled with my new look, since my sister was so thin, she saw my weight as a sign of health, never realizing that I was using it to console myself from the intangible feeling of instability hanging over us in what appeared to be a normal life.

My mother was hard on me. She only disciplined me, since in her mind I was the strong one, the healthy one. My sister was allowed almost any kind of privilege or indulgence, to the point of breaking my toys and dolls. I remember vividly how she broke the furniture in my doll house, ripped the legs off my dolls and broke my doll buggy. I happened to be very neat, and cherished my toys, so I became furious when her destruction spilled into my realm. I hit her quite often, and my mother would descend upon me with the wooden spoon, avenging my sister's screams. It seemed to me that my sister was permitted to do anything she pleased and nobody could touch her, whereas I was harshly disciplined for the most minute infraction.

These feelings of being squelched and controlled became a running theme for me in my childhood during World War II. I had a relatively easy time in school until I got into the third grade. I still did fine academically, but I started to get the strange feeling that my teacher had it in for me. During the first and second grades I had teachers who had a positive attitude towards me. They were elderly ladies who actually remembered teaching my grandfather with fondness, which carried over to me, and I blossomed. By the third grade, things were changing even in our little world, and we were feeling it. I had a teacher of the "new guard", who was envious of the status our family-at-large still enjoyed in the community, notwithstanding the new era. Of course, I did not make this connection until analyzing it much later in life. At the time, I just had a gnawing feeling that she was against me, but I had no idea why. My family was upstanding and well liked still, but as the war waged

Chapter 1 | Czechoslovakia 1934-1945

on and news of what was happening changed from minute to minute, some of the best in people came out, and yet others began turning on each other. This one third grade teacher chose me as the target of her frustration, apparently. One time she ridiculed me in front of the entire class in a very sarcastic manner with regard to an assignment which I had misunderstood. I was openly upset and she quickly saw where she could get at me. I did okay in math but I was not crazy about it, and it was in this area where she really cut me down, for an entire school year. I lost all my confidence and really did become bad at math. Unfortunately for me, she also taught our fourth grade class the following year. Her son was in my class too and she babied him embarrassingly. He was a mama's boy. Two other children were singled out by her besides me. One was the son of a Nazi family with whom she had been friends with before the war but now no longer spoke to. The other was the son of a non-Nazi aristocrat. He received the roughest treatment because he had a terrible time adjusting to the public school system. In the earlier grades he had private tutors at home. He was an extremely bright student but our teacher made no effort to accommodate him. She was the most authoritarian teacher of my school years. Our principal was a Nazi madman who later committed suicide after the regime fell.

I felt totally surrounded by "absolute rulers": my extremely authoritarian schoolteachers, my disciplinarian-mother, the highly structured, rigid Catholic religion in which I was raised, and the totalitarian Hitler Youth, which every German youth, age ten, had to become a member of. Luckily I experienced the latter for one year only. The only oasis in this desert was my grandmother, with her love, her hugs, and her delicious food. My grandfather was also a tough guy figure, but for me, his dominance felt more removed than the other threatening personalities in my life.

By 1944 everyone was beginning to feel the effects of the war. There was a food shortage that was not as acute for my family, because my father's sister owned a grocery store and helped us out a lot. But clothes and shoes were hard to come by, and everything was distributed by means of coupons. Often, we had coupons but no merchandise was available.

It was the beginning of the end of World War II.

Tishi REFUGEE • IMMIGRANT • MOTHER

Anneliese, the pampered only child

Above: Anneliese and little sister Inge with their mother and father (home on brief leave) in 1941

Chubby Anneliese who turned to Grandmother's sweets, with her mother and sister in 1943

Chapter 2

The Russians and the Czechs

The year 1945 was chaotic. The schools closed in November 1944 and were first turned into refugee camps and later into barracks for the retreating German army. In March and April of 1945 we heard the thunder of the front coming closer and closer. During the night, the sky was red in the distance, and our fear grew day by day. Strafing runs by the Russian fighters were advancing toward us, and we had several mild air raids. Strafing is when an enemy attacks repeatedly with bombs or machine guns from low flying aircraft. Although the siren would sound and we took cover, all through April we breathed sighs of relief because the planes never seemed to get that close to our town.

Then one day in May, we had a serious air raid. It was 7 o'clock in the morning, and this time the demeanor of all the adults was different. They weren't hysterical or panicked, but they also were not trying to make it fun for us, as they had previous times. We were told to run into our basement. After the first wave of danger had passed, my mother grabbed my sister and me and ran, along with many of our neighbors, to my grandfather's sizable wine cellar, which had been designated as one of the community air raid shelters.

It became very crowded in the shelter with children crying and old people groaning, but soon we all settled down and just waited to see what might happen. It became a day of saturation bombing. The waves of bombers came at half hour intervals, and whenever there was a lull during which we thought we could relax from the rain of high dropping bombs, the strafers would come with their hail of machine gunfire. As the day went on, this pattern became thoroughly established. Once in awhile, the door of the shelter would open during a quiet period, in order to let fresh air in. I had decided that we were probably going to die, as it became clear that there was to be no quick end to the raids. I was almost eleven years old. Every time the door was opened I lifted my head (we were laying on the floor of the shelter on our stomachs) and looked to see if the house on the hill across from the shelter was still standing. It was, and every time I saw it, I got renewed hope that we might survive. The bombing lasted until 7 o'clock in the evening. It was pure luck that we lived to see the next day. When, after 1 a.m. no more bombers were coming, we timidly ventured out to step into the street. The sky was bright red in one area and we later learned that the candy factory where my grandfather had worked had been hit and was on fire. Everyone decided to retreat back into the shelter to spend the night, since it was dark and no one knew what condition their homes would be in. There were two more strafing raids throughout the night, but the major bombing had stopped.

The next morning we saw the extent of the destruction. We could not believe our eyes. We put a white flag at the shelter door and waited in the street to see what would happen next. I had avoided looking in the direction of the house on the hill across from where we were.

When someone from a nearby shelter came running to tell us that the Russians were here, I finally looked up to see if that house on the hill was still there, and it was, but it was not intact. I didn't know how to feel.

No one knew what to do. We just stood around waiting for some help, or some instruction, but nothing happened. Slowly everyone just started to go back to their houses. I remember being stunned by the devastation I witnessed. On the way home we saw one house totally demolished. Later we learned that the family had been in the basement and they were all dead. Windows were broken and roof tiles blown away on most of the houses still standing or partially standing. There was no electricity. When we arrived at our house we just cried. All the windows were blown out and some of the roof was gone. The apartment house

Chapter 2 | The Russians and the Czechs

behind our family dwelling had been a direct hit. Half of the structure was obliterated. Luckily the tenants and the German soldiers in the basement had survived by running to the side of the structure that remained, however two soldiers were not so lucky. They didn't make it to the other side in time and were buried. It took days to dig them out and in that time they were crushed to death beneath the weight of the rubble.

May 8th, 1945 the war was officially over in Europe. As a child, one adapts to new situations, and I must admit, my sister and cousins and I did find the Russian occupation exciting. Our house was taken over by a group of officers that promised no harm would come to us. My mother became the heroine of the neighborhood. Whereas she was normally a person who tried to be inconspicuous and unobtrusive, she now symbolized strength and action to our neighbors. Most of them were afraid to stay in their own homes and wanted to come to our house since we had the Russian officers with us.

A number of women and children moved in with us and it got quite crowded. We were permitted to keep our bedroom and kitchen. The officers occupied the rest of the house. Thus, everybody was crammed into one bedroom. We slept on the floor, together in beds, wherever there was room. Safety was more important than sleep. We all took care of each other.

A lot of looting and raping was going on all around us. Young girls and women were dressing like old ladies with big scarves hiding their faces, in order to be left alone. The Russian soldiers started getting drunk at night and shooting off guns for fun. It was frightening. Yet one day the officers told us they were moving out, and we realized how vulnerable we would be without them there. We began frantically looking for a safe place. My mother went out in search of shelter for us and to find the rest of our family. She went to my grandfather and aunt's house (they lived together in a large two-family structure). She found it empty, with broken glass everywhere. The front door was broken down and the house looted. She kept looking for her in-laws and found them, along with the rest of our extended family, hiding in a farmer's cowshed. She asked if they would allow my sister and I and a couple cousins and their moms to join them.

Our quarter of the cowshed, which was actually a small barn, was the horse stable. It was somewhat removed from my cousins, but grandfather slept near us during the night to protect us from intruding Russian troops. There was a Russian farmer's son who had also taken up residence on that farm. He was simple, but a good natured person. At first we were unsure of him, but he promised to protect us. In time, we realized he sincerely meant what he said.

One day the Russian troops withdrew from our town. We wanted to move back into our house again but the Czech government forbid us to. My one aunt's house had taken a direct hit by the bombs, so we moved into the two-family house of my grandfather and my other aunt. After we cleaned it up a bit, it was inhabitable. We were permitted to stay there until early July.

During the period we lived in that house, my grandfather was taken on many occasions to be interrogated by the Czechs. Sometimes he was absent for two days, brought back home, taken again overnight, and then brought back home again. After approximately a three day lull, he was taken away again. This pattern continued on a regular basis until one day, they just stopped coming for him. I asked my grandmother if he was going to stay home and she said yes, he was back to stay, and that he was in the bedroom. But she asked me not to bother him, as he needed his sleep. I somehow managed to get by her and sneak in to see him and I was horrified. He was unconscious, with bruises all over, and a swollen, bluish face. I snuck around trying to listen in on every adult conversation in the house, trying to find an explanation, which I soon overheard.

Grandfather had been beaten by the Czechs during the last interrogation. He was shown a picture of himself greeting Hitler's troops with the Hitler salute. He was made to kiss the swastika on a big Hitler flag. He was then beaten severely by the same Czechs whom he had helped by getting them light sentences with probation- for sabotage during the Hitler years. I am not aware what their act of sabotage consisted of, but I do know that Grandfather had obtained a reputable attorney for them and that the attorney and my grandfather were sympathizers covertly

Chapter 2 | The Russians and the Czechs

with the Czechs that were on trial. These were the same Czechs who had just beaten him bloody.

I presume he was beaten for his leadership in the freedom movement for the German people, which he started after the first World War, when he had helped attain the right for Germans to vote, among other privileges. I presume that in the Czechs view, by promoting the cause of freedom for Germans in Czechoslovakia, he should also be blamed for aiding the arrival of Hitler's troops.

In early July, we were told we needed to vacate my grandfather's house. We all had to leave quickly and move into an empty house which formerly belonged to a German-Jewish family. No one wondered much about where they had gone, since much of the town had emptied out, with people going in search of relatives, especially once the Russians had left. This time each family had a whole room, and we all shared a bathroom and the kitchen. My grandfather cried the day we had to leave his house. I had never seen him cry in my life. Even though he had healed on the outside from the beating, he always seemed like a broken man after that.

We tried our best to adjust to our new living situation. Meanwhile, my uncle came back from a Russian prison camp with a shaved head, looking like a skeleton. My 16 year old cousin also returned from his "Hitler-Youth Fighting Duty" with ghastly stories. Life had hit a very low point, where we all lived each day in fear. In order to mark us, the Czechs made us wear an "N", for "Nemec" or "Nemka" which means German in Czech. We had an 8 p.m. curfew, forced labor with no pay, and soon, one male after the other was taken off to prison. Our house became a household of only women and children.

One day we were informed that all German children were to report to the Czech public school closest to them and attend classes. My cousins and friends and I arrived with mixed feelings, joining the other German children waiting, not knowing exactly where to go or what to do. It was an alienating experience to have teachers speaking Czech only, in the same classrooms where German-only had been spoken a few months before. Our little stint in the Czech school system lasted only three days. Then we were told to stay home. There was to be no school for German children at all. My cousins and I stayed at home with my grandmother, who did the cooking for all the members of the household. Our mothers all had to work. There was little food and I began to lose weight. My over-indulged taste buds underwent a radical adjustment. Grandmother felt badly that she could not cater to my desires anymore.

My little sister accompanied my mother to the various forced labor duties she was assigned. One job she had was inside a barn, working with hay. After several days of being there with my mother, my sister developed a severe breathing problem. We had a family friend who was our personal physician. He was a kind Austrian doctor and came to our house to examine my sister. She was diagnosed with asthma. He gave her some medication and did not charge my mother anything. Because of this incident my mother, who felt the need to keep my fragile little sister by her side, requested to be re-assigned to some other type of work. We were pleasantly surprised when her request was granted and she was sent to a Czech family that had a huge orchard and vegetable fields. My mother enjoyed this type of outdoor work and received kindness and concern from the lady of the house, who treated my mother and sister very well. She saw our family not just as Germans, or the enemy, but as individual people. She fed my mother and sister hearty meals, and I was allowed to come along sometimes as well. She also gave my mother food to bring home. Unlike many who knew us, but acted as if they had never met us, this woman remembered our family fondly from the pre-Hitler days. She said she remembered us being good and generous people in the community.

When the cold days of winter, 1946, set in, and the work outdoors ended, my mother was not re-assigned to another work group. She was able to stay home with us. My 16 year old cousin was released from imprisonment by the Czechs/Russians, and we were hoping things were getting better.

Chapter 3
Becoming a Refugee

Near the end of that January in 1946, the word came suddenly that we should pack one suitcase per person and report to an old school building. We had no idea what would happen to us, but imagined the worst. We thought we were being sent to a concentration camp for extinction, as we had heard terrifying stories of such things happening to Germans.

The old school building we had to report to had been converted into a camp. Straw mattresses were on the floor for sleeping purposes. My sister suffered terribly from the hay and dust in the room. We met a lot of our old friends and the adults were all actively engaged in guessing the meaning of the entire operation.

Our stay in that camp lasted about ten days, at which point we were loaded onto a truck and shipped to the railroad station. There, we were loaded into a freight train that was waiting for us. Our car had the luxury of a little wood stove in the middle of the car with a pipe through the roof directly above. Czech soldiers with submachine guns and bayonets supervised the loading, and shut and bolted the doors when the train was ready to leave. We went short distances with stops in between, but had no idea what the stops were for because we could not see anything. We were laying on the floor in a mix of blankets and old potato sacks for bedding. The wood stove barely kept us warm. There were full sacks of potatoes in the corners that we were instructed not to eat from. During one of the frequent stops, all of a sudden, the door was opened, and

Tishi   REFUGEE • IMMIGRANT • MOTHER

we were ordered to come out and walk around a bit and urinate in the bushes. The Czech soldiers stood at the ready with their guns, herding us back into the car after a few minutes. We noticed that the train had grown into an endlessly long snake and that we had picked up a lot of other wagons on the way. This explained the many stops. Our journey continued, once the doors were bolted again.

We adjusted to the pattern of morning, noon and night stops. The doors were opened and we were given a minimum amount of bread and coffee, then instructed to relieve ourselves in the bushes, with the soldiers always there, holding their menacing weapons. They wanted us to keep quiet, do our business and get back on the train. During one night of horror, we made a stop, and before we got off the train, someone's babies in the crowded car would not stop crying. The soldiers grew agitated and my mother, my sister and I, along with others, hid behind the sacks of potatoes that were sometimes placed on the train for periods of time, then removed. The babies suddenly stopped crying, a woman screamed, and everything became silent. It was dark and hard to see, and we did not want to see. At this stop no one got off, the doors simply closed and the train began moving again. After a long time when it felt safe to talk, those of us hiding emerged. We were told that two babies had been stabbed with bayonets by the soldiers, and then thrown from the train. No one in our car made an attempt to escape. After a week of traveling in fear, the door was opened one morning and the Czech soldiers were gone.

We saw German civilians instead, and American MP's, without their guns pointed at us. We were told that we had left Czechoslovakia and were at the border checkpoint, in Germany.

Years later I learned that this was called "The Expulsion", the solution to getting rid of Germans in other countries after the war, particularly those of Eastern Europe, and those under Russian rule, like Czechoslovakia. Our family was one of millions displaced at the end of the war and carted into either what would become West or East Germany. Many Germans didn't make it through the trip and died of cold, disease or starvation. Others were bayoneted to death for trying to escape, or simply making a wrong move. I'm not clear on how it was decided which of

Chapter 3 | Becoming a Refugee

us belonged to East Germany, behind what became known as the Iron Curtain, and which of us became part of West Germany.

At the checkpoint, we had to undergo a disinfection procedure during which a powder was jammed down our necks and backs with a disinfectant gun. We were then loaded back on the train, and when we pulled into the city of Bayreuth station, the doors opened once again. It was explained to us that the train would be dismantled, and that different cars had different directives, to different destinations. We learned we were going to be part of a six car train that was going to Kulmbach. Kulmbach was in what we would come to know as West Germany. In Kulmbach we were greeted by the German Red Cross and civilians. No soldiers of any nationality were in sight. The atmosphere was totally relaxed and we were treated like human beings. We were still in shock and did not trust the situation. I remember feeling frightened about what would happen next. After over a year of intimidation we did not know how to act. We could not comprehend that we were free to talk and walk normally without interference from authority.

Instructions were given, stating that our quarters would be inside a castle on top of a very steep hill in Kulmbach. The castle was called Plassenburg and was quite large, however, we were joining and to be joined by, hundreds of other refugees. Some were Sudeten like us, and others were from Silesia. Sudeten Germans had resided in Czechoslovakia, the Silesian Germans came from Poland.

It was cold in the castle almost all the time. It was February, with a lot of snow and extremely cold weather. My mother, my sister and I were allotted one corner of an alcove with a window, with our one suitcase each. The corner was the size of a tiny bedroom with cots jammed together. The castle was serving as a refugee camp and had terrible refugee camp food. The food was of low nutritional value. Our menu consisted of coffee, thin soups and a half slice of bread per person, per day. Our treat from time to time was goose fat.

We had no idea where my father was or what the future would hold for us. I was disoriented and depressed. My mother enrolled me in the higher educational system in Kulmbach. It was a two mile walk from the castle to my new school. I was already exhausted when I got there in the morning. The accent of the native population sounded foreign to me and after more than a year of not attending any school, I had no idea how to fit into a school system. I considered myself a bored visitor. Most refugee children from the Plassenburg camp went the lower educational route, so there were just a few other refugees in my school. I became a loner. The school preferred for the students to go home at noon for the mid-day meal and then come back to school afterwards. This meant an additional trip to and from the Plassenburg. By the time I was home after school, I was so tired I had no intention of doing any homework. I developed a detached attitude toward the educational process.

In German schools at that time, religious instruction was part of the public school curriculum. Protestants and Catholics had separate instructors. I was assigned to a Catholic priest who was a monster. We had him once a week. He practiced the most dogmatic Catholic creed on us with bloated self importance. He inquired every week who had not been to church on Sunday, and whoever admitted that they had not been, got hit forcefully with a wooden stick on the palm of their hand. He also required his students to go to church one time during the week. The church was one mile away from the camp. So on certain days this involved me climbing the steep hill to the castle three times. It was physically strenuous but it was better to comply than be singled out in class and punished. I was quite a compliant person at this time because I still had the fear of the Czechs and the Russians in my bones. One time I almost passed out in church and a friend quickly took me outside. The incense was too overpowering on my empty stomach. I lost twenty pounds in those trying months. Looking back, I asked myself, why did this priest never come and minister to the people in the camp who needed moral support? Why did he choose instead to stay in the classroom, behind the pulpit, and in his comfortable parsonage? There were hundreds of displaced people who felt frustrated, desperate and isolated. They could have benefited from his encouragement. It was a sobering thought, and the beginning of my disillusionment with organized religion.

The native population of Kulmbach began to resent having all the refugees dumped on their neat little town. The town had somehow

Chapter 3 | Becoming a Refugee

escaped the air raids and was totally preserved. Even though the people did not have much to eat, due to the total breakdown of the entire country, Kulmbach citizens were coping relatively well. We felt like intruders in their calm little world.

The other freight cars on the refugee train had been diverted to a town called Ulm. My father, who had been a prisoner of war with the Americans, was released at Darmstadt, and headed for Ulm to look for us. He had connections in Ulm because one of the female Air Force volunteers where he had been stationed in France, had her home in Ulm. Later I learned that he had had a relationship with her.

He went to the Red Cross in Ulm to inquire about us but found no answers. He also walked through the refugee camp there, where he met some people who had come from our town of Misslitz and had been on the same train. They told him that we might be in Kulmbach. My father went back to the Red Cross to check it out. After some inquiries, they informed him that this was correct.

My father went to a dental supply house in Ulm after his refugee camp visit, to see if the owner had any idea where he could find work. The owner of the dental supply house, Herr Anbele, said my father was a lucky man because right at that moment he had the wife of a dentist sitting in his office. She was looking for someone to rent her husband's dental practice since he still was unaccounted for and she needed income. My father met with her and explained his background to her, how he had just come out of a POW camp, and that he was penniless.

He asked if they could work something out, and they came to an agreement. He would take over the practice and also live in her home, splitting the proceeds heavily in her favor, as rent.

She also knew that he was going to come for us, and that she would have to find room in her home for his wife and two daughters.

One day in June 1946 my father walked into our camp. We could not believe our eyes and were incredibly happy. After the initial joyousness, my mother became uneasy. She was partially relieved but also had some anxiety regarding my father's return. She had just started job hunting and had two potential prospects. She was about to arrange our

Tishi   REFUGEE • IMMIGRANT • MOTHER

life accordingly. She had found some lodging for us downtown and also had an old boyfriend who she had been seeing. I did not like him at all.

Though my mother anticipated life with my father at the family helm again with mixed emotions, we did go about gathering our things together and we did join him in a little town called Erbach.

Chapter 4
Rebuilding: In and Around Ulm 1946-1949

Erbach was a quiet little village outside the city of Ulm, where my father had rented his dental office. Frau Pappelan, the lady of the house, had converted a room in her basement into a kitchen for us. Her daughter's room served as a bedroom for our entire family. Her daughter was an adult and lived there with her boyfriend, staying in another bedroom. The boyfriend and my father got along quite well. There was a lot of male bonding going on with much talk about the war and their shared experiences. This may have been great for my father's ego, but it was of no comfort to my mother, and did not help any bonding between my parents, who were still somewhat estranged from the wartime separation, and their respective romantic interludes with other people during that time.

The area of Southwestern Germany that we were in is known as Swabia, which is part of Bavaria. But the people of Swabia have a strong dialect and their own culture. My transfer into this culture was an even greater shock than life at the camp in Kulmbach had been. In the country town of Erbach, as in Kulmbach, there was no damage from air raids. Yet, the nearby city of Ulm was over 75% destroyed. The center of the city was one giant pile of rubble. The railroad station, which served as a hub for many lines, consisted of hastily erected wooden barracks. The people were hungry, and dressed in mismatched, shabby clothing. In Ulm, as refugees, we were resented much more than in Kulmbach, but for different reasons. Since the population of Ulm had nothing themselves, they felt that we were invading their territory and taking things away from them. Many of the city people started a pilgrimage to outlying country towns and went begging at farmhouses for food. The farmers out in the country resented us as well, preferring to help their neighbors from Ulm, instead of giving us, as refugees, any breaks or discounts. We felt alienated and displaced, and although my sister and I weren't exactly close, we did become closer going through these hard times together. Unfortunately, although it was clear they still loved each other, my parents could not find much common ground anymore, and the hardship only made them more distant from one another.

During this period of my life I felt like alienation just followed me. In school, where all the students spoke in Swabian German, even the teachers had a Swabian singsong sound, like a chime, in their voices. I was actually reprimanded for my special accent, which, at the behest of my mother, was actually what is considered in Germany (land of a thousand dialects), to be "high German". I did have a slightly Austrian sound, but I certainly spoke more correctly than most of the people in the area. There were only about two to three refugees in each classroom of about 30 to 35 students. Once more, the majority of refugee children went to the lower educational and trade school system. At that time one had to pay tuition for the higher educational system. Most refugees could not afford this, but my thrifty mother always made education a priority and would skimp on other things in order for her children to attend the better schools.

I just felt out of touch with everything, including my teachers and my fellow students. The teachers didn't do much to make the sprinkling of refugees feel at home. I was having a hard time adjusting to school as serious business, since I had experienced so many interruptions in my schooling. One incident in particular sticks in my mind.

In the morning, school didn't start until 10 a.m. The group that came to school by train from the villages arrived at 8 a.m., and I was one of them. Having finally made some friends that I usually sat and had coffee with during that time, I came up with a great idea to really connect with them. At my initiative, we all went to the Ulmer Münster, which is a beautiful Gothic Cathedral, and was miraculously, still stand-

Chapter 4 | Rebuilding: In and Around Ulm 1946-1949

ing. We climbed the circular staircase leading to the top of the church steeple, known as the highest church steeple in the world that one can climb. Our excursion caused us to be late for class, in fact, we were an hour late. The teacher was furious, which shocked me because I thought she would consider it an educational experience. There is a local saying: "In Ulm, um Ulm und um Ulm herum", which, translated into English means, basically: "In Ulm, around Ulm and all around Ulm". The German version of course, rhymes, and is somewhat of a tongue twister, which is why it was, and still is, a funny and popular thing to say when people come to Ulm. I thought my teacher would appreciate that I had taken my friends to see all of Ulm and more, like the saying, and I told her so. Of course I was living in my own dream world to feel that way, because I was still totally disoriented. Her move was to call on me to recite the times tables, which I did not know, and did not feel obligated to know, given what I had been through. I did not feel bad about taking the girls, or not knowing my multiplication, but I did not like looking stupid. The teacher told me to study hard that night and I did. I came back to school the next day and recited the times tables 1 through 20 with no mistake. She was pleasantly surprised. Two days later she called on me to recite them again, for a student who had forgotten, and then suddenly, I myself, found my mind a blank. The teacher was absolutely astonished. She could not believe I had forgotten everything in two days, but I had. I could not believe it myself, but it actually happened.

At this point I started to address myself more seriously to my schoolwork. I tried to study, but I had a difficult time concentrating or retaining much long term. I ended up with low marks in a rigid educational structure. My home life was not conducive to studying. My parents still did not get along well, owing mostly to the relationship my father had with the woman in France during the war. From listening to their arguments, I gathered that my mother simply could not get over it. I found it strange, since she herself had started things up with an old beau she had met up with again in Kulmbach, but I kept my mouth shut about it. My sister's asthma had flared up and my mother was busy with her, and trying to feed a family, when all of Germany was experiencing deprivation of all consumer goods. My father saw dental patients all day and then did his own lab work at night. No one in the family had time for me.

I befriended a girl by the name of Elisabeth who is my friend to this day. She was the daughter of the mayor of the village of Erbach. Her father had been appointed as mayor by the Americans, since he spoke English well, and he had to cooperate and work with them. He actually was a high school math teacher.

Elisabeth and I quickly became close friends since she had as much trouble as I did, relating to people our own age. Her father, while brilliant, was domineering in the house, to the point of being chauvinistic. Her mother was a sensitive and shy person, and living with Elisabeth's father put her under terrible stress. Elisabeth was afraid of her father because he was like a dictator toward her and the rest of the family. He was sort of neutral toward me in the beginning. Later, he had times when he approved and disapproved of me, depending on where I was in my development. Much later, when my interest in politics crystallized, he and I had long discussions about the Russians, the Americans, government and other subjects, and we still have them to this day whenever I get back to Germany.

My disenchantment with my teachers, my family and the native Germans continued, as did the poverty of the population in general. We had galloping inflation until 1948, when The Currency Reform Act was carried out. For one day, all Germans were equal. Our money was wiped out. It had become so worthless, people had wheelbarrows of Reichsmarks to buy one loaf of bread. I never saw this, but heard that prices were so high, and goods so scarce, that in some places this happened. The Soviets, as the Russians were now called, and the Americans, issued Germany new money. I don't remember how much we received, but every family got the same amount delivered to them in the form of a new currency called the "Deutsche Mark". Eventually, larger denominations of old money could be exchanged for these Deutsche Marks, which we later called D-Marks or just DM's.

Economically, things moved rather quickly after that. To everyone's surprise, the store shelves filled up with merchandise. All the while we had thought Germany's supplies had been decimated, when actually,

Chapter 4 | Rebuilding: In and Around Ulm 1946-1949

merchants were hoarding goods in warehouses, waiting to see what would happen, afraid to sell and receive money that had no value. Within a year, the economy was up and rolling again, but there was a clear line drawn between the haves and the have-nots. Established German businesses flourished, but for dentists who were German refugees from Czechoslovakia, it was still going to take a bit longer to build back up to the status we had once enjoyed. We belonged to the have-nots.

Meanwhile, during 1947, the man of the house, Dr. Pappelan, had returned from the Russian prison camp he had been in all that time. He was weak and emaciated and did not intend to work right away. He was in fact, bedridden when he first came back, but we knew our days in his house would soon be over. We began our search for new quarters. Even though all German natives were forced by the government to take in a refugee family and share their homes and apartments with them until they were able to afford their own home, it was not easy finding the right fit. Many families had already fulfilled that edict; and then there was the matter of finding a place with enough space. But by the time Herr Dr. Pappelan had regained his strength, we had secured a place nearby to stay.

We did not have to move very far. We shared a common bedroom again, all four of us, and our kitchen was a room with the bare minimum of kitchen equipment: a wood stove and running water. My father was now unemployed and we were living off our savings. We went collecting pine cones in the woods for our wood stove, as well as berries for jam. We loaded all of this onto a wagon every day and lugged it back to our place. I actually preferred these outdoor tasks in the fresh air, over doing my homework. So I fell into a habit of not doing homework, and having now made more friends at school, I just copied from one of my classmates in the morning.

My father of course, once again, went about trying to re-establish himself, but this time in his own right. He applied to the Organization for Dentists in Germany. They assigned dentists to an area where they were needed. There was no opening in Ulm, where I went to school, so my father started considering the countryside again. There had to be a certain number of people per dentist in a given area, so that there would not be too many dentists in one spot and none in another. Naturally, everyone would have liked to work in the city, with access to so much more than in the country.

After much persistence on my father's part, he was finally admitted to a location, and it was another small village, only one and a half miles from where we lived. It was sometime in mid 1948 that he started to work there, with only a minimum of equipment and a lot of determination. He traveled by bicycle at 7 in the morning, arriving at 7:30 and starting in right away with his first patient. He saw patients all day until 6:30 p.m. Then he got back on his bike, rode back to Erbach where he had his lab in a different place than our residence. I had to bring him his supper every night, which he ate in the lab. He got home from doing his lab work every night at midnight or later. This kind of schedule was hard on all of us. It went on for an entire year. Eventually we were able to move into our own apartment in Dellmensingen, the town where he had his office. After a while, he was able to move his lab into the office building.

We finally had an apartment of our own. It had two bedrooms, a living room, a kitchen and a toilet. No bathtub. In order to take a bath we had to go down to the basement and bathe in a big washtub, but it didn't bother us at all. This situation was better than anything else we had lived in for a long time. We were very happy with this new set up.

Meanwhile, my grandfather, who stayed behind in Czechoslovakia, had been held in prison all this time, although my uncle and cousin were freed just before our departure. There had been a lot of interest in him, because he was a political figure. In late 1948, he was finally released and found his way to Kulmbach, where our remaining family had stayed, establishing roots there. The refugee camp had been dissolved after most of the people left, scattering throughout Germany to meet relatives. Some stayed behind in Kulmbach, as part of my extended family did. My grandfather was supposedly bought out of prison by his son-in-law's Czech family. My father's sister had married a Czech, who had renounced his Czech background and joined the Germans, however, he had remained in close contact with his family.

He became a pilot in the German Air Force and crashed his plane in

Chapter 4 | Rebuilding: In and Around Ulm 1946-1949

a fog over Poland during the war. Our family took care of his family's needs in Czechoslovakia during the war, and after the war, they took care of ours, by helping Grandfather get out of jail. After recovering physically, he started to organize the German refugees, and in 1949, when Germany split apart, and set up new governments, he ran as the candidate for the refugees, the BHE party, which was short-lived and dissolved into the SDP or the CDU, the two main parties evolving in 1950's West Germany, also known as the Federal Republic of Germany.

He was elected to the Assembly in the Bundestag (similar to the House of Representatives), and became friends with Konrad Adenauer, who was our first post war Chancellor, when they both served on what was called "The Council of the Elders". My grandfather was re-elected until 1954, when the rearmament of Germany was being debated in the Assembly. The pressure proved to be too much for the man who had been through so much, and he suffered a stroke during the debate. After a short hospital stay, he was rushed from Bonn to Kulmbach by his chauffeur. The hope was that being home around his family, he would recover. Sadly, he never regained his full abilities and was in the hospital in basically a vegetative state for a year. He died on July 20, 1955, just three days shy of my 21st birthday, which I was already celebrating on a four day trip to Paris. He was 76 years old, and unaware of the "economic miracle" his friend Chancellor Konrad Adenauer helped create for his country.

Tishi   REFUGEE • IMMIGRANT • MOTHER

The Tichi family reunited after the war: thin, shell-shocked and struggling

Right: The family, robust and thriving, after the Currency Reform Act and release of goods and services (1949)

Anneliese's grandfather, RIP

Chapter 5
Moving into the Fifties: Of Boys and Men

By 1949, heading toward 1950, I had become more integrated into my school life in Ulm. I had three close friends and felt a kinship to my classmates, but still with some reservations. I had matured physically very early. My period had started a couple months before my 12th birthday, back in 1946. I became interested in the opposite sex at an early age, and by the age of 14 in early 1949, I had a crush on a boy who was 16. I was emotionally immature, and although we did kiss once or twice, nothing else materialized. Soon I developed another crush on a young man, approximately seven years my senior. He was extremely charming and had a way with the females, both older and younger. He actually had kissed me once when I was 12, and by 14, I felt tortured by all the attention he gave other girls. Everybody liked him, and he flirted with every pretty girl he saw, which almost killed me inside. He always talked to me but then cut it short, acting as if I was too young for him. It annoyed me very much. He finally took real notice of me when I turned 16. I was so happy that after all those years of suffering, I finally had truly caught his eye. He supposedly became my boyfriend but kept right on flirting with other girls too.

Between 16 and 17 my suffering continued, because I considered myself "of age" but I was unable to capture his full attention. He became well acquainted with my parents, and enchanted even my mother, but nevertheless, I sat many a time without a date at home because he was "busy".

Tishi   REFUGEE • IMMIGRANT • MOTHER

By the age of 14, I had started to take my Catholic religion seriously, finding in it, an escape from my misery. But by the time I became 16, strong doubts as to the validity of it all had developed in my mind. I did not find comfort or solace in prayer because my prayers went unanswered. I never got any response from God in any of my prayers. I don't mean a response in the sense of my wishes and desires being granted. I mean that in spite of all my attempts to communicate with a supreme being, I simply never felt any comfort in return, no relief. I kept hanging in there though.

My Catholic upbringing also resulted in the repression of my sexuality, which was certainly trying to arise in me, and had been for quite a while. Besides passionate kissing, I never got involved in anything else. I believe now that at least heavy petting would have been indicated and appropriate at 16, but my Catholic education and my mother's puritanical ideology did me in. My mother spoke only in euphemisms about bras, panties, menstruation etc. In fact, back when I did get my period for the first time I did not have any clue what was happening to me. I thought I was dying! My sister and I never had any form of sexual education. I did not know what a homosexual was until I was 17 years old. The act of sex itself was a total mystery to me until I finally lost my virginity at the age of 20. Before that, I was totally IGNORANT in that area, and that was probably why my so called boyfriend sought the company of other girls.

On the one hand I wanted to preserve myself for marriage, for this great, unique experience that it was all supposed to be, On the other hand, from what I could gather about it, I did not want to do this dirty thing with anybody. The Catholic Church and my mother had succeeded in keeping me chaste at the expense of what I now consider a healthy attitude towards sexual fulfillment.

When I was 17, I finally gave up on my boyfriend and gave him his walking papers. I also saw the movie "A Streetcar Named Desire". After seeing it, I feared that if I got sexually involved with a man, I might go crazy, whether I was married or unmarried. I was afraid the experience would be unbearable and I might go insane like Blanche DuBois. I talked to my girlfriends about it and they looked at me with disbelieving

Chapter 5 | Moving into the Fifties: Of Boys and Men

eyes. My mother's Puritanism and the Catholic Church had done a good job on me. I still was terribly drawn to men, but made a pact to myself to keep things flirtatious and friendly, but not sexual, until maybe one day I felt stronger and thought I could handle it.

Around this time, our all-girls school arranged dance lessons with an all-boys school. I got quite a male following and was invited to many dances our schools had. All the attention I received on these occasions made up for my disillusionment after my breakup.

Near the end of our relationship, my boyfriend had introduced me to an acquaintance of his, a young medical doctor who was doing his residency in Ulm. He was ten years older than I, and I was flattered when he began to come around after he found out I was free. He was very good looking, and my parents were pleased by his station in life. In the midst of enjoying this new man in my life, I found myself overpowered with emotion for him. It worried me that when I was around him I suddenly could not think straight. His good looks and his prestige and all the attention he paid me swept me up like a hurricane. He was very Catholic, and his entire demeanor indicated that he had honorable intentions. I used to get scared at times, wondering if he was going to ask me to marry him. Despite all his positive qualities, I had a gnawing suspicion that at some point I would not be as serious about him as he was about me. And then one day he did ask me, but he wanted to know if I minded waiting until he had established himself in his medical practice. I said "No, of course I don't mind", quite matter of factly, like a 17 year old girl would. As suddenly as I had been overwhelmed by him, I realized I was not what he was looking for in a wife. He wanted a demure little housewife who would be cooking, sewing, taking care of the children, and remaining naive about the world. I did not give up my friends or even my flirtations to be with him, and one day he told me he had been mistaken about me. He said I was a little tree which still had a lot of growing to do. I said that was fine, turned my back on him, and went into my family's apartment. That was the last I ever saw of him.

On the one hand, I was relieved that he dropped out of my life. On the other hand, I felt humiliated that he had dropped me and not the other way around. I also had to put up with my family and friends who were dumbfounded. At that time, my ideas about not wanting to be the typical German "Hausfrau" would have sounded nuts to them. After all the war and postwar trauma, no one would have understood why I would not want that security. Everybody kept asking what happened. I simply shrouded myself in silence.

In 1950, something wonderful happened. After four years, Czech refugees of German heritage were granted German citizenship. All that time, we had been without an official country.

It was a great feeling for our family.

Meanwhile, I developed a correspondence with a cousin of my father's. She was a nun in Vienna who had obtained her doctorate in philosophy before she entered her order. She was involved in writing books about the Catholic saints. For that purpose she had to travel to Paris to do research at the libraries there, and on her way, stopped off in Ulm and came to see her cousin, (my father), and his family in Dellmensingen. She was a kind woman and I soon developed a liking for her. I told her about my doubts regarding the Catholic religion and its claim to being the only true and right religion. Our stimulating discussion continued on through letters, and we corresponded until it came to a halt when she wrote me that at some point things cannot be explained, but must be believed. And that is where we parted ways. I simply could not believe the various dogmas the church had set up, and I chose to personally ex-communicate myself. I had tried very hard to believe, but it just didn't work for me.

So, at almost 18, I had no boyfriend, did not feel a connection with my parents, had practically no relationship with my spoiled sister, gave up my religion, had a befuddled idea about sex, did not like school and was depressed. I did have my three girlfriends though. How thankful I was to have them!

At this point in the German educational system, one could continue into higher education, learn a trade, or leave school.

One of my girlfriends intended to go to the French part of Switzerland and work for a French family to improve her grasp of the language.

Chapter 5 | Moving into the Fifties: Of Boys and Men

It sounded like a wonderful idea to me, and I told her I wished I could do something like that. Within a short time, she became homesick, but had endeared herself to the family she was working for. The lady of the house, Madame Chalier, told her to write a friend to come join her, that they had plenty of work, since it was just herself and her husband on a large estate. It was not much pay, but room and board, and a chance to really speak French and have an adventure. My parents were uneasy about it, but I convinced them that it would be less stress than formal schooling, and I explained to them that their continuous fighting was not a conducive environment for me to find peace in. They reluctantly agreed, and I found myself with my friend Regine, in a little village outside Geneva, called Versoix.

It was a beautiful place, right on Lake Geneva. In clear weather I could see the tip of Mont Blanc. Madame Chalier made us work very hard, and was a temperamental lady. As I mentioned earlier, she and her husband were the only inhabitants, besides Regine and I, of what was called "Villa de Castelon". They had a wine wholesale business and were quite well to do. Regine and I learned about wines and how to drink them and pair them with dinners, which we took to, quite well. We disliked the amount of intense housework we had to do, but figured it was a small price to pay for such an opportunity.

My parents read between the lines of my letters and demanded that I come home after three months because they felt the work I was doing was too much for me. I did not want to leave and was determined to stick it out an entire year, but since I was not of age, I had to respect my parents wishes, pack up and go home. Regine's parents thought it was a good educational experience for their daughter to stay, and I think they were right. I felt that my own parents were overly possessive of me, which at 19, I despised.

Once home, my father offered me work as his receptionist and assistant, since the girl who worked for him was pregnant and would be leaving soon. I wanted to go to the Language Academy in Munich and study English and French in order to become a trilingual secretary or translator, but my mother would not let me go. The excuse was supposedly a financial problem, yet they were about to build a large house. I

35

felt like they just wanted to hold onto me.

I tricked my parents into a deal. I agreed to work for my father, but told them I would be saving the money for my tuition at the Language Academy in Munich. My father agreed to take care of my food and rent, and I was supposed to save for Munich, not spend anything on clothes. My mother agreed too, since she knew my fondness for nice clothes, and expected me to be unable to resist.

They did not count on my determination. I put the main part of my pay into a savings account, wanting so badly to buy some new clothes, but not giving in. After a year and a half, I finally had the money for my tuition to study languages. I could not wait to get away from my parents. My mother was shocked, but she had to put up with the fact that I was going. I was 20 by then, but it was still hard for her to let go.

While I had been working with my Dad, my cousin, who lived in a suburb of Munich, had invited me for a weekend to attend a dance at his fraternity. A very impressive young man danced with me all evening long, letting his fiancée sit alone through every dance. At an impressionable and self absorbed 19 years of age, I reveled in that attention. I enjoyed that event tremendously. I told the young man I expected to be living in Munich within the year. Back in Dellmensingen, I kept receiving flowery letters from him and when my Dad had to go to Munich on business, I came along. I went to register at the Language Academy and to spend time with Francois, as he liked to be called. He was actually German but had some French lineage in his family that he was very proud of.

He met me at the Haus der Kunst in Munich, a well-known art museum. We took a walk in the Englische Garten, and then he boldly invited me to his apartment. He told me he had broken off his engagement, that it just hadn't worked out, and not to worry, that it was not because of me. He was 28, and had just finished his law studies. I went to his place, he made coffee, we talked and soon he became quite amorous. I found him extremely attractive. He was eloquent with words, and I found myself falling for him. We got involved in some very heavy petting and if I had not had to meet my Dad at the train station, who knows what might have happened. I had the hardest time remain-

Chapter 5 | Moving into the Fifties: Of Boys and Men

ing faithful to my principals about not having sex and keeping myself sane.

I met my father at the station in an agitated state. Luckily for me, he was with some other people and didn't notice. He was engrossed in lively conversation with them, which gave me some time to straighten things out in my mind. By the time we arrived home I had collected myself, and even my mother, who was the more observant one, didn't pick up on anything either. I told them how great the Haus der Kunst museum was and what an interesting exhibit they had been showing. I told them how Francois had met me there and how we had taken in the exhibit together. That seemed to satisfy their curiosity.

In the fall of 1954, my mother took me, her 20 year old first born daughter, to Munich, to enroll in the Language Academy. She had found me a family to stay with. I had a room, and use of the bathroom. My meals would be at the school or out, and I had an allowance to work with. My mother helped me get set up, then left for home. As soon as I was alone I contacted Francois by phone. I was disappointed. He said he could not see me for two days because he was busy.

I started school and waited for him to get in touch with me. He finally came to get me on his motor scooter, but dropped me at a sidewalk cafe, saying to wait for him, that he just had some business to attend to. I waited for 2 hours and when he came back he said he only had time to drop me back off where I was staying. I was so letdown! He promised to get together with me in two more days and said that he would have more time. I did not understand his actions.

In two days, he came as promised, on a warm September evening, at a time we had agreed upon. I was happy that he was punctual and affectionate and all my previous concerns were forgotten.

He drove me to an outdoor Biergarten where we settled down to a cool glass of Munich beer. We talked and he became very affectionate. He told me how happy he was that I finally lived in Munich, and then he continued to flatter me in so many ways. After awhile he suggested we go to his apartment. We had another beer at his place and we talked some more. His bed was skillfully made up to look like, and serve as, a couch. He became extremely intimate and told me he would like to make love to me. He was very bold because I think he knew instinctively that I was going to have a hard time turning him down. He was seductively insistent, yet without pressure. He was quite confident and sensuous and knew exactly how to turn a female on.

I, however did not cooperate in the way he expected. I immediately became unromantic, fighting my internal urges, and very matter-of-factly explained that I was saving my virginity for marriage. His answer was that marriage is love's burial ground. I also inquired about his ex-fiancée whom I knew he saw occasionally still. I asked if it was really true that I had nothing to do with the break-up. He said no, the relationship had run its course anyway. We proceeded to talk about love, life, virginity and relationships for two more hours, with him and his experienced hands weakening me as each minute passed. Finally, I decided to just give in. I felt comfortable with everything he said, and I decided I was in love with him, and if I did not make love to him, then I do not know to whom I would. It felt inevitable at this point, and very healthy.

It was painful and messy and not the great romantic experience I had expected. On account of the physical evidence (my body's reaction was to bleed), he saw that I really had been a virgin and was honestly taken aback and quite surprised. I felt hurt that he had actually doubted me. The bleeding did not stop for days and it frightened me terribly because I could not tell anyone or get advice. I was so ignorant in these matters. I finally concluded that the sex had triggered an off schedule period and that was what was going on. Another month later confirmed it, since the next one came right on time according to this new schedule. I had contact with Francois during this time and confessed my fears to him. He tried to reassure me that it would be fine and it was. I felt a lot better after things got back on schedule and my body returned to normal. I had made it through my first sexual experience and had kept my sanity.

In time, however, my conscience started to gnaw at me. I started feeling guilty about my actions. I thought that everyone could see on my face that I had lost my virginity. I felt very low at times. But when I was together with Francois I forgot all my doubts. Whenever we went

Chapter 5 | Moving into the Fifties: Of Boys and Men

to his apartment he wanted to make love to me. He said I had a "natural talent" for it. What he didn't understand, as I sadly had to admit to myself later, was that I was very much in love with him, and my "natural talent" was pure devotion to him.

It seemed to me from a certain point on that he wanted to make love to me all the time. Whenever we were together it was his main concern. I started to get irritated and told him that there were other interesting things to do besides having sex. He did not agree and said that his fiancée had been terrible in bed, and that was the reason for their break up.

I became more and more dissatisfied with the role I was playing. I wanted a loving boyfriend who did all sorts of activities together with me, not just sexual encounters. I decided to play it cool, but my heart was sinking, because it was becoming clear to me that he only wanted me as a plaything.

At the same time, I was busy with my schoolwork, which distracted me in a good way, but also kept me from resolving the situation with Francois. I just put up with it and concentrated on doing well at the Language Academy, devoting a lot of time to my studies.

We had a new student start about two months into the first semester. She had black hair, was dark complected with big charcoal eyes, and she had a sensuous mouth that she accented with bright red lipstick. She looked beautiful and mysterious and I was drawn to her out of curiosity. I thought she was from Turkey or Greece, but it turned out she was from Poland, and she was Jewish. Her name was Hanka. We became friends, and she often came to visit at my place and I to hers. Her older sister was a medical student at the University of Munich and Hanka lived with her. Sometimes we did homework together, sometimes we ate together. I hinted that I had a boyfriend without telling her that we were having sex, or how much I was committed to him, or how much I was in love with him. She told me she had a terrible crush on a young man who was about to emigrate to the U.S.

Christmas 1954 came, and I went home for the holidays. Nothing had changed. My parents were still fighting, my sister still held center stage, and I almost left before my vacation was over. I could not take the obnoxious environment.

Tishi   REFUGEE • IMMIGRANT • MOTHER

Back in Munich, my relationship was cooling. I felt hurt and unhappy, holding on to my boyfriend for dear life, hoping against hope that things would straighten out. They did, but differently than I expected.

Near the end of January, our school had it's annual "Faschingsball" at the Regina Hotel. Fasching is like a mixture of Halloween and Mardi Gras. I made myself a sexy little costume, and invited Francois to the ball. I introduced him to Hanka and he caught fire at her beauty. I acted like I could care less, but inside I was steaming. Hanka acted reserved towards him. He then invited everyone to come to his apartment after the ball. A funny thing happened at the dance. One of our young teachers turned out to be a friend of Francois. His name was Charlie Fischer. They had gone to school together and acted like long lost friends. Charlie, as we called him, reported all the virtues I displayed in his class to Francois, who seemed pleased, but not as impressed as I would have hoped. I was basking in the attention, yet Francois did not seem focused on me.

A group of people, including my cousin through whom I had met Francois, and whom I had invited to the dance, went over to Francois' apartment. Hanka had left with Francois ahead of the others, which really irked me on his part, not hers, since I had not made it clear that he was my boyfriend, nor that I had strong feelings for him, or that we were involved sexually.

The evening turned into a boring night of drinking at his apartment and we stayed late but left disappointed. Hanka and I left together and went to her sister's place. Her sister was furious with us. She had woken up at 6 a.m. and Hanka had not been there. We actually arrived at 7 a.m. by streetcar.

Subsequently, Francois and I had little contact for awhile. Charlie Fischer invited him to a get-together our class was having with some American friends of Charlie's, so we could practice our English. Francois spoke English fairly well so it made sense. Naturally he came, and of course, he ignored me and only had eyes for Hanka all evening long. He asked her if he could meet her and she said o.k., but that if he was not punctual she would not wait around. Hanka, by the way, had fallen

Chapter 5 | Moving into the Fifties: Of Boys and Men

hopelessly in love with Charlie Fischer. And I mean hopelessly, because Charlie was tremendously adverse to male-female relationships. I heard it rumored later that he was homosexual. So Hanka went to meet Francois at the agreed upon place and since Francois was always late, she left. He tried to ask her out again, but she refused, since she was not interested in him anyhow.

The Fasching was at its height and Hanka and I agreed to meet Francois and a friend of his who I decided I might like, at a restaurant. It was not a date, but a group thing, yet when Francois showed up with a female companion and not the friend I liked, I made an embarrassing scene. Francois left with his companion and that was the end for me. I lost all interest and did not want to see him anymore. I told Hanka everything.

After the Fasching was over and Hanka was at my apartment one day, Francois just showed up. I wasn't sure who he wanted to see, but I saw it as a perfect opportunity to officially end our relationship. Before I could begin, he reproached me for my behavior the last time we saw each other. Hanka kept saying "don't take anything from him, don't even listen..". I asked her to leave for a while, since I had unfinished business with him, and she obliged. I then was alone with Francois, who tried to use his lawyer skills on me. I told him to be quiet and listen to me, and I proceeded to explain to him why I did not want anything to do with him anymore. At first he objected, but then he realized I meant what I said and there was no changing my mind. I was completely uninterested and done with him. He left, pecking a kiss on my cheek. Three weeks later he sent me a postcard from Vienna inquiring how I was. I did not respond.

Unfortunately, after the Francois experience, I had another experience that made me feel lower than I did already. It was with Hanka. She had told me once that she and her family had been in a concentration camp, but since she never spoke any more about it, I did not bring up the subject. At that age, and at that point in time, my knowledge and understanding of what went on during the war regarding the Jewish people was limited to hearsay and coffee talk and occasional official news that was murky. I knew that awful things had happened, in fact, it became clearer and clearer to people my age. But at the time, nothing was taught about it in German schools. They just made reference to the fact that Jews were put to work in camps and moved on. Of course we asked questions in and out of school, but our elders were vague with answers. By 1955 though, I knew about the SS, Hitler's special police, and I knew they had done terrible things.

Ever so often we would go to a bohemian area of Munich called Schwabing, to a conversational club where people from all walks of life came to practice their English. Our academy recommended that we go there. I had been there several times with and without Hanka. This one time, she was along, and we sat at a table with a group. I overheard one man say that he had been in the SS and I just turned on him. I had never actually seen anybody that had been in the SS, but I knew they had most likely committed all sorts of atrocities in the name of Germany. I always felt angry for having to share the German guilt without having hurt anyone, just being a child batted around by the war myself. My self-righteous indignation just bubbled over and burst out of me onto this man. I was all worked up and did not consider how Hanka might feel. I angrily began telling him off for committing terrible crimes, to which he answered "I only followed orders, I had to follow orders."

Hanka jumped up and ran down the stairs into the street. I ran after her but it was obvious she wanted to be left alone. She ran like crazy. I felt bad. I had not thought of her, I had only thought of releasing my own vengeance on that SS man. I went home too.

The next day Hanka was in school. She told me she ran all the way home and told her family what had happened. They all got upset and stayed up late that night talking about their life in the concentration camp. I felt even worse than the night before.

Hanka said, "If the Germans were permitted to do it all over again, the same thing would happen." I protested, telling her my generation was more aware, and would never support any movement that directed acts against others. I told her we would not be as ignorant or desperate ever again. I asked her why she lived in Germany if that is what she really believed. She said everything I said made sense but that I could

Chapter 5 | Moving into the Fifties: Of Boys and Men

not understand how she felt because I was German.

This incident wrecked our friendship. It drove a wedge between us. I became defensive, trying to point out and prove how good Germans could be. She became bossy and domineering towards me, obviously taking her feelings about the Nazi's out on me. We both became resentful. We gradually saw each other less and less and finally refrained from having anything to do with each other. I was unhappy about the demise of our friendship, but I realized something. On that day in Schwabing, even though I was mad at the SS man, she still saw me as the enemy. From that moment on, the situation was hopeless.

After the debacles with Francois and Hanka, I became depressed again. My schoolwork suffered too. I still did my work, but I felt like I was living in a fog. I felt cheapened and mistreated and I had a very low opinion of myself. I just didn't see any value in myself.

In the spring, Charlie Fischer, who was a mountain climber, took whoever wanted to come along, on an outing into the mountains. He had a friend of his along by the name of Toni.

Toni paid a lot of attention to me, and I was quite receptive to any male attention. I talked to him a lot during the outing and found him refreshingly honest, simple of character, and natural. He was the total opposite of Francois.

Charlie Fischer had paid attention to me too, and I even went out with him for a glass of wine, but he was so reserved he made me uncomfortable.

Toni was a blue collar worker who took English in night school at our academy at Charlie's suggestion. After the trip in the mountains I sometimes met him after night school and we went out together.

The end of the semester came and I went to Paris with a bus load of professors and students from the Polytech Institute. Our school was originally supposed to co-sponsor the trip but pulled out at the last minute, and I had already registered. Thus I was allowed to go with the Polytech School. I spent four days in Paris with a bus load of strangers, but learned everything one can learn about Paris in four days, and celebrated my 21st birthday there. One of the professors knew every nook in Paris and spoke French perfectly. It was an uplifting experience.

When I came home I learned my grandfather had died, and I was sad, but relieved for him, because it seemed his life had become only about stress, and was no longer joyful.

The rest of that summer I stayed home, and other than writing a letter to Francois and receiving a response, I don't recall any major experiences in that time. I wrote a letter to Francois telling him how I had enjoyed Paris and that Paris sent its regards to him. We had originally talked about planning a trip to Paris together. He answered, telling me how the quality of my handwriting seemed deteriorated and that I did not seem to convey any of my old vivaciousness through my writing. Basically, he wanted me to know, that he knew, he had wrecked me. I wondered why I had bothered, thinking maybe I did just want to show him that I could go to Paris without him and have a wonderful time. Since my motivations were suspect, even to me, I decided to let the matter be dropped.

In fall, back in Munich, I had to start preparing for grueling final exams in February. I found studying for exams difficult and had a hard time concentrating, with no special excuse. It was just hard for me to concentrate and Toni tried to help. He was very supportive, urging me on. I also got sexually involved with him, which Charlie did not like at all. It hurt his odd feeling of purity, but then again, as it turned out, he had other, latent feelings going on. I think he actually cared for me too, but did not know how to express those feelings.

Having been raised with an underlying anti blue-collar attitude, I wanted to test the ideas implemented in me by my family, and found the perfect situation in Toni. I did make it through my final exams, but in the process I had to admit, I grew somewhat tired of Toni. He bored me. He was a simple man of black and white and right and wrong. I tried to theorize with him about more complex ideas, but he was unaccustomed to that kind of thinking and shut me out.

I met with Charlie to discuss what I should do about Toni, who was, after all, his friend. But somehow that meeting ended with Charlie and I kissing, and that complicated the entire matter.

I graduated from the Language Academy of Munich and applied for

Chapter 5 | Moving into the Fifties: Of Boys and Men

a job, which I managed to get, although I was terribly bored in that first position. After only four weeks, I applied for another job, and this was a fairly nice office, but rather demanding work. I was working for an American insurance company as a bi-lingual assistant and secretary. The work involved typing, shorthand, composing memos, talking to people on the telephone and in person. Doing most of this work in English so suddenly, I found it to be extremely challenging. All the employers were German, as well as our boss. The big boss in Frankfurt was American. Whenever he showed up we were on high alert to perform our best.

In my personal life, I had gotten rid of Toni, told myself to forget about Charlie Fischer, and engaged in a series of four short-lived liaisons during the spring and fall of 1956, one of which could have led to marriage, if I had wanted it to. I was however, not prepared to settle down into a position that, to me, would have outlined my life clear into retirement, and left no surprises. Munich was a wonderful place, but to live there the rest of your life, knowing what was lying ahead, was not adventurous enough for me. I wanted to marry someone who would be willing to live abroad, work abroad, travel a lot, and be of an open mind towards other cultures and other places.

Tishi   REFUGEE • IMMIGRANT • MOTHER

Anneliese at one of her dances, a standout in bright white (early 1950's)

Anneliese with one of her men

Chapter 6

The Winds of Change

One day in September 1956, a first lieutenant of the U.S. Air Force strolled into our office and wanted to file a claim for his clothes and belongings that had been stolen when someone had broken into his car while he was on vacation in Italy. He walked to the other secretary's desk, since I appeared to be busy. He kiddingly asked both of us why we were not out going for a walk on such a beautiful September day. Our boss was sitting right there too, and one just does not say things like this in front of a German boss. I thought to myself, "This guy is crazy," and went on about my business. Three weeks later he was back checking on his claim, for which we only covered the broken window. This time our boss was not in and the atmosphere was more relaxed. He talked to the other secretary about his claim, and I left the room to get something. When I got back to my desk, he was sitting in front of it, and tried to engage me in conversation. He said he wanted to go out with one of us, but that the other secretary said she could not because she was in the middle of getting a divorce. He wanted to take me to Schwabing and I told him I had seen everything in Schwabing there was to see. He then mentioned the Fuerstenfeld-Brook Officer's Club, which I did have a strong desire to see. However, I had promised my mother that I would never go out with an American and I felt that I should keep my promise. I had so many German friends, it never occurred to me that I might have trouble keeping that promise. My curiosity won out and I said I would come along. He said he would call me before our date, which he

47

made for over two weeks away. As the time came close I decided I would not go, and that he would probably forget anyhow.

The day before our scheduled date he called and I felt put on the spot. I said yes, I was coming, but I became scared. I did not know this man, nor did I know anyone who knew him. I was apprehensive. While I was getting dressed, a fuse blew in my apartment and I could not find my landlady. I knew nothing about fuses myself. I had to get dressed by candlelight, which took a while, and I was hoping he would give up on me and just leave and be gone. It was getting rather late by the time I was ready. When I came downstairs, there he was, still there, just leaning against his car, but he admitted he was about to get in and take off. He was surprised and happy I showed up, saying he had almost given up on me. I explained about the fuse and the candlelight and I apologized. I got into his car and we drove away. We were talking, but I sat in the corner of the front passenger seat pressed against the door in case he should attack me. I had heard many newspaper accounts of German girls being harmfully attacked by American servicemen. The drive to Fuerstenfeld-Brook seemed endless. At times there were no houses, no lights, we were just driving in the country. We finally arrived and I felt myself relaxing, being among people. The waiter seemed to know him, and I deduced that there had been other females before me that were introduced to the club. This did not bother me, in fact, I felt a bit more safe. He ordered fillet-mignon and I ordered the wine, a Chateauneuf du Pape, which I got to like very much when I lived with the French couple near Geneva. We had an excellent dinner and a great time. We talked about Arizona, where he came from, we talked about rattlesnakes, male and female relations, my family, all sorts of things. The most remarkable thing was that I could be totally myself without feeling that I had to put on airs. And he was so wonderfully unpretentious and natural. I wished this evening would never end, but it did. We arrived at my place at one in the morning. Somehow, I hesitated to get out of the car after I had said good-bye, and he must have felt I was waiting for something more, when in reality I just did not want the night to end. Unfortunately, he misinterpreted my hesitancy and started to be intimate with me. I was so shocked one could have thought I was a virgin still. He immediately

Chapter 6 | The Winds of Change

pulled back and I went home quickly. The agreement was that I would call him if I felt I wanted to continue to see him, since he already had said he wanted to see me again. But I had to think this over. One interesting, exciting date to the Officer's Club was one thing, but to go out with an American was quite another. My family would not tolerate it. Now, however, I did not think I wanted to see him again anyway, after this experience. The next day was a Saturday. I did not have to work, so all morning I weighed the pros and cons in regards to calling him. Then I thought about the marvelous evening we had together and I got the warmest and most pleasant feeling again. By 3 p.m. I called, and he was so happy. He had apparently been concerned about me possibly never calling at all. We went out that night, and ended up at his nice apartment.

My girlfriends grew jealous of my new "friend". They could tell we had a great time together. We started to see each other all the time. He picked me up after work, we ate together, and soon, we slept together. This was an entirely different feeling than any of my previous interludes with men. We quickly became serious about each other. We spoke both English and German together, but I liked to practice my English so that is what we spoke most of the time when we were alone. Even though he had learned to speak reasonably decent German, Lynn still had an American accent and just could not say my name properly. He started to call me by my last name, which was really what most of my friends called me anyway: Tichi. The funny thing was, he couldn't pronounce that correctly either. It ended up sounding like Tischi, the American spelling being: Tishi. I liked it.

Christmas 1956, I had to go home. He drove me to Ulm and was somewhat hurt that I would not take him to my family in Dellmensingen and introduce him. I tried to explain...but he did not understand. He went back to Munich and I took a train from Ulm to Dellmensingen. Nothing had changed at home. My parents were still fighting and my sister would sound the alarm to me when things got particularly hot and together we would help cool them down. Except for feeling closer to my sister, I did not enjoy myself in the tense atmosphere. After Christmas was over, I tried to broach the subject of my American. I told them that I had almost brought a boyfriend along from Munich, and he was not German. I saw them visibly stiffen. I continued, adding that he was an American Lieutenant of the U.S. Air Force. An earthquake began rocking the house. If I had said he was the devil himself their reaction would not have been any different. They wanted me to quit my job in Munich immediately and come back home. My father said he would go and see my boss about it. I answered that I was 22 years old, and he wasn't going to do anything, because legally he had no right. I felt put under tremendous pressure. I do not understand their attitude to this day. Nobody seemed to care about my personal life all that much while I was with them, and now suddenly, presented with what they perceived as the threat of losing me, they behaved like crazy people. My Dad pleaded with me to forget this man, saying he would lose all his patients if I married an American. I said I wasn't marrying anyone, yet, at least. I hadn't even been asked, I told them, and besides, people didn't really care about things like that anyway.

I returned to Munich thoroughly depressed at my immature and unworldly parents. My American had been afraid that I would never come back, for some reason. When I did, he had some friends over that I did not care for, but thankfully, they left in a hurry. I was depressed about my parents and depressed about him inviting idiotic people to his place. He said he did not care who he was with, he just needed to be around people because I had left him at the train in Ulm in a state of turmoil.

After we spent time together, we both calmed down and things did not look so threatening. I explained my family's reaction to the fact that I had an American boyfriend. He could not believe his ears. He had been in German family's homes before and had never encountered such prejudice. I wondered if it was because my dad had been held prisoner in an American POW camp, a time he did not speak about, at that point, except to other soldiers.

By January 1957, I had a lot of belongings in Lynn's, my American's, apartment. My office was on the way to his air base, so he dropped me off in the morning and picked me up on the way home. I mostly stayed at his apartment. We had been discussing marriage, and I felt by staying at his place I was compromising my position. He had been engaged to

Chapter 6 | The Winds of Change

a German girl before, and she had dumped him and thrown his ring in a river. He was wary of my situation with my family and especially uncomfortable with the fact that I would not introduce him. He said he needed more from me before he could ask me to marry him. I started to move my belongings back to my apartment when he wrote me a beautiful love letter. And he spelled my nickname the German way..

Lynn's letter:

1230 hours
17 January 1957

Dear Tischi,
Just a letter-and what you read here will no doubt make very little difference in the future. However, sometimes, when I am thinking so much and so strongly about a certain subject, to write it down relieves me and even helps produce a solution. So, here goes.----

You are quitting--you are leaving, and we will not see each other again. That is a number one fact that causes me to worry so much. Number two fact is me--I --what I want. You are leaving because you think our relationship has an impossible position for you to maintain, that the future does not hold the foundation that you desire for your place in society. You have mentioned many times that marriage with me would not be any different than what we are living now, and as far as certain feelings and actions between you and I, you are right. What we have had together, I can truthfully say, I've never had before. On 30th November, 1956, we had our first date and it has been just 49 days since then, and I have had experiences during these 49 days that I will never forget. And they are all about - with - over - a girl named Tischi --- Tischi ---Tischi.

In trying to compare these 49 days to their importance with all the other 49 day periods of my life, it makes me sad and a little lonely and even ashamed of how little all the other periods meant.

Last Sunday night in the middle of the road, you said you were so happy you had met me. Actually I had to fight the feeling I had, then. I wanted to propose to you, and then I remembered how short a while

51

we had been together and that there would, in certainty, be other times. Today it appears I was wrong. I hope you have not changed in your feeling of having been glad to have met me. I say this because, regardless of what happens in the future - I am glad and happy for the short time we were together. I have the feeling in my heart that I would do anything in this world --- anything --- to make the time we are together to 49 years instead of 49 days. But, then, I am a human, and a man -- and maybe -- as you would say "bloody damned stupid."---And as a man I hold these inalienable rights. The things or action I could take very quickly to make you stay by me, I probably won't do. Why,---? I can explain it only by closing my heart out and looking directly at the problems of marriage between us. There is a strong possibility that you would feel always as a stranger or foreigner in my land, even though you say you can be international. Everything one says, he cannot always do, and I would like to see a portion of this type of adaption exercised. I believe if anyone can be this way, you are the girl that can, but I still want to see it. So many people and things will hurt you in America. You will not be able to see them all here --- and if I told you, it would be too unrealistic and of no value. When you are hurt there, you will feel yourself that I am your only connection --- this will not be really true, as in America, everyone, every citizen, has a relation to the entire country that gives the individual the rights to carry out life as he or she desires. Well, I talk and talk and think and think. The decision I reach is that you and I should be together and that we (neither of us) should force the time or ways but only that we love one another, understand one another and in the future have some kids together.

Considering marriage at present, the "anti" feeling is too great within me. It is not desire for others, it is not lack of desire to be married, --- it is only the feeling of time --- time for knowing the trueness of our relationship. Previous experiences have sharpened my feeling toward a "true-type relationship" to a razor's edge.

Stopped here and re-read this whole letter and Tischi, it sounds just like a corny output of a poor young man in love, and in reality,-- that's what it is. I hate weakness and a man in love is weak. If the girl loves him also, then the man becomes greater than a mortal. This must

Chapter 6 | The Winds of Change

close here --- and whatever we do, let us hope we don't regret it later.

You have my love Tischi
Lynn

I finally agreed to have him meet my family. He immediately proposed. I had wanted him to, but the reality of what this entailed was staggering. I said I had to think it over but then accepted after not much deliberation. By the end of January, we started on the paperwork. When I saw how many copies of documents we had to fill out for the Air Force alone, just to get the marriage application, I did not want to get married. I left it all to Lynn. We also went to get our wedding rings, which, according to German custom, are worn by both parties on the left hand. During the ceremony, they are switched to the right hands. We had our wedding rings and carried them around in a little box, since my parents had to be worked on before our engagement could be known.

My dad came to Munich. He had finally consented to meet Lynn. They had an amiable discussion and my dad's appraisal was: "He is nice, but a little tall." (Lynn is 6'3"). Well, I was certainly happy with the result, but now, we had to work on my mother.

We were aiming for February 15th, since this was my dad's birthday, which provided a good reason to visit my family. So, on February 15th, 1957, the great confrontation took place. My parents would not permit us to come to the family home. Instead, they met us at the hotel near the railroad station in Ulm. They were ice cold to us and we felt like leaving, but we stuck it out. Then we went to a restaurant in a different area, more out in the countryside. The hostility continued through dinner. We almost left again, and they became concerned, at last, making an obvious attempt to be civil. Finally, when they saw they could not split us apart, they decided to invite us back to the family apartment in Dellmensingen. Once we were all there, they became much nicer, actually hospitable and pleasant. We had brought gifts for my Dad's birthday, which he appreciated very much.

Lynn spent that night at a local hotel, I stayed with my family. They pleaded with me not to go through with the engagement and marriage,

53

but I remained steadfast. On the 16th we socialized with them and took my sister for a drive. She was totally enamored with Lynn, and ended up being a big supporter for us.

On the 17th of February, 1957, my parents finally gave their approval and we wore our rings. The wedding was set for May 11th. We were told it would take those three months to get all the papers approved by the American military. Meanwhile we had to get all the other papers in order to have an official German wedding together. At that time there was a lot of red tape involved in getting two people of different nationalities married legally. When we had completed all that paperwork we had a two inch paper stack in our possession. We had to laugh at the ridiculousness of that.

In April, oh fright, I decided I must be two months pregnant. I was petrified because of my family. I knew they would be inconsolable, and I was afraid they might disown me as their daughter. I figured this would just be too much to take.

I tried to find a doctor who would perform an abortion, but first of all, in 1957 it was next to impossible to find someone like this. Secondly, the minute I explained that I was getting married, everybody thought I was crazy to want an abortion. Nobody seemed to understand the fear I had of my family. Everyone insisted they would be ok with it.

Lynn and I decided to keep the baby but to keep it a secret until as long after the wedding as we possibly could. Aside from doctors and clergy I had consulted, no one else in my world knew anything. It was between Lynn and me.

Chapter 6 | The Winds of Change

Excerpt from Tishi's manuscript

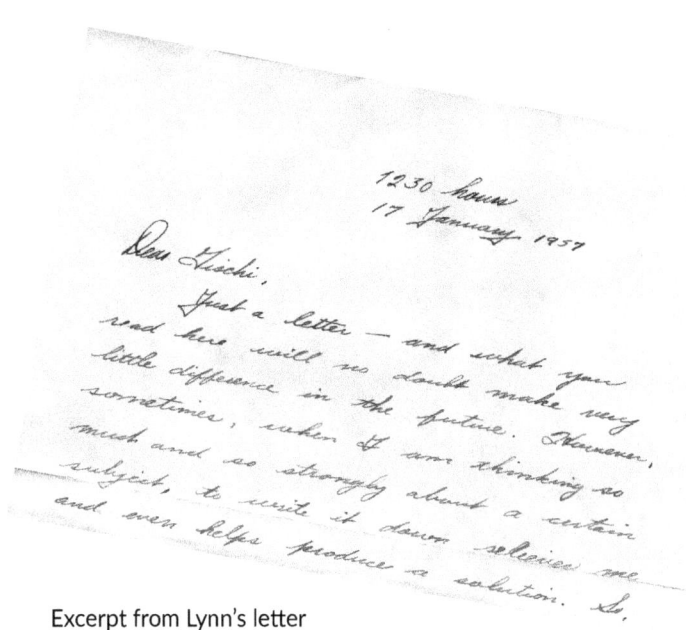

Excerpt from Lynn's letter

Tishi REFUGEE • IMMIGRANT • MOTHER

Chapter 7

Love, Marriage and America

My parents gave me a big white wedding. This was not something I wanted at all, not being one for pomp and circumstance. I went through with it for them, in order not to hurt their feelings. It did not take place on May 11th as planned. The documents from the Air Force had been delayed a few more days. On May 15th, 1957, we were able to get married. I was scared stiff and so was Lynn. We were undoubtedly in love, but this kind of a commitment seemed awesome to me.

We had a ten day honeymoon on the Italian Riviera in Alassio. It was before the official season so we were spared the tourist hustle-bustle. We had a wonderful time with moments of pregnancy sickness interspersed. We swam, we ate, we went shopping. We drove to Nice in the sunshine, stopped in Monaco and lost $25.00 gambling. We stopped in Revo and ate dinner. The weather was lovely. We watched the sunrise from our balcony. This trip constitutes one of my life's most pleasant memories.

Back in Munich, I moved into Lynn's apartment with my remaining belongings. I had retained my job and stayed with it until July. We moved to the outskirts of Munich, close to the air base. We settled in on the top floor of a two family house. The downstairs was occupied by Lynn's Major who was a strange kind of fellow. Luckily we did not have much contact with him.

Lynn was expecting his orders to come. He knew it was time for him to be shipped back to the U.S. He had extended it as long as he could. Directly after the wedding I had applied for a visa to the U.S. and was

Tishi   REFUGEE • IMMIGRANT • MOTHER

hoping to get it in time to go along with my new husband. I had the fear that if I stayed behind my family was going to scoop me and my baby up and keep us in their arms, smothering us. That's the feeling I always had about them.

The orders came. Salina, Kansas. Lynn was disappointed. He had hoped for a more interesting assignment. It really didn't matter, since he wanted to get out of the Air Force anyhow and go back to school for his master's degree.

We made arrangements in August to have our car shipped back. Our blue blue Ford. I have such fond feelings for that automobile. I stayed with my parents while Lynn drove the car to Bremerhaven. He came back and we took the train to Munich. My parents had been very nice. They did not argue for once, they were a team consumed and united by their feelings for me. They felt that they were losing me, I could tell. My mother came to Munich to help me pack. She ended up doing all the packing, making me rest. She was so concerned about me. It touched my heart.

My parents were not as intolerant as I thought they would be, about the fact that I was pregnant. This was largely because we did not tell them until June, and although we did not lie about how far along I was, we did not offer it up either. And they did not ask. Since I exercised, I had tight muscles and was not showing much at all. It also turned out, I had a small baby. By June it must have seemed like there was no point in being mad; after all, I was married, which met their standards of propriety.

Once our things were shipped from Munich to the U.S., we went to Dellmensingen for a few days. Then we were supposed to be in Frankfurt on September 29th. My parents came with us to Frankfurt where we said our final goodbyes. I was glad when it was all over because my father acted as if he would never see me again. My mother behaved rather bravely. She hardly cried and when she did, somehow it did not bother me. Little did I know, that actually would be the last time I saw her. It was all straining, emotionally draining, and I was relieved when the pressure eased.

My parents left to go home to Dellmensingen and then it turned out

Chapter 7 | Love, Marriage and America

we had to wait in Frankfurt for twelve hours to take our flight. There was a tremendous storm over the Atlantic.

Our flight lasted 20 hours. We flew on a propeller airplane. The whole thing was quite pleasant. We arrived in New York City at eight in the morning.

Idlewild Airport was one mass of shoving and pushing people. It took us some time, but we found our luggage and were assigned to a bus, which took the entire U.S. military crowd from the airplane to an assigned hotel in Brooklyn. I was terribly tired by this time and we were given a dirty, dusty room on the top floor. We refused to take it and were told there wouldn't be another ready until noon. When we returned at noon we were told to wait. We waited until 3 p.m. before we could finally sleep in a bed. The next day we went to see if our dear blue Ford had arrived and it had. We were given access to it and spent a few days sightseeing, from the Empire State Building to the Statue of Liberty, Broadway and shopping in New York, with rest periods in between. We were giddy with excitement and our energy seemed to regenerate continuously.

At last we embarked on our long road trip to Arizona to see Lynn's family, with a stop in Salina, Kansas to drop off some of our things. I was 7 months pregnant and finally feeling it. I grew tired easily, yet I enjoyed the road trip tremendously. I found Gettysburg, Pennsylvania fascinating. West Virginia was beautiful but so poor. Kansas was just plain boring. Lynn had been right. Now I understood why he had been disappointed. I was disappointed too.

Our trip went on, and the further west we went, the more excited I got. I felt like I was on another planet. I had never seen any place as desolate as the Texas panhandle. Hardly a town along the road, just tumbleweeds and red sandstone, absolutely magnificent. Coming from overcrowded old Europe, I felt like we were driving through a fairy tale. I kept saying "Where are all the people?" By the time we came to Arizona I had gotten accustomed to the empty spaces, but Arizona's unique beauty was breathtaking. I experience the wonder anew, every time we go there.

Tishi REFUGEE • IMMIGRANT • MOTHER

Our reception in Douglas, Arizona, at my in-laws was...very nice. I had a bit of a shock when my gentlemanly husband arrived home. He greeted his parents, brothers, cousins and friends, introduced me around, definitely with love and pride, but then disappeared. I was left with a mother-in-law who eyed me suspiciously. The next thing I knew, Lynn showed up with his buddies on horses, in jeans and a cowboy hat, saying he was going to be gone for a couple of days and his mother should teach me how to cook Mexican food! It was one of his favorite food types, since they lived near the border and he had grown up eating it. Off he went, this cowboy version of my Air Force Officer.

His mother did teach me wonderful Mexican recipes in those couple of days. But she was distant, and considered me "the foreigner" who had somehow tricked her prince of a son into marrying me. I felt guilty, like I had to prove myself innocent. After all, I was pregnant, and I also had developed a vaginal infection, which was treated by the family physician and caused more grimacing and disapproval from my mother-in-law. As much as I loved Lynn, I felt abandoned and wondered what I had done. Who was this cowboy? Where was my elegant husband? Thank God for his Aunt Jewel, a real gem of a person, as her name reflected. She welcomed me with open arms, as did Lynn's father, a gentle, retired railroad engineer. Aunt Jewel owned a beautiful ranch, and in the ten days we spent in Arizona, I got to know what ranch life was like. Lynn returned and was understanding and supportive. One of his friends also had a ranch and he took me there, too. We just ate and drank and talked during that ten day whirlwind. Casual ranch life was a totally new dimension for me. Lynn had two brothers, one of which was a railroad engineer like his dad, because he had grown up during the Great Depression, and did not want to financially burden his parents with college. Lynn and Lee, the other two, both were college graduates.

I could not get over the informality of western life, as opposed to the formal kind of background I came from. The ten days passed and we started our way back to Schilling Air Force base in Salina, Kansas. To this day, I make marvelous frijoles, guacamole, tacos and a Mexican casserole my family raves about.

Back in Kansas, we rented a disastrously messy house from a sergeant

Chapter 7 | Love, Marriage and America

whose wife had left him. He had no use for an entire house. He had lived in it by himself for awhile and it was very dirty. I set about with soap, water and a brush, and started to clean. By the time I got to the bathroom, I was so nauseated from all the filth that I started to vomit and simply could not clean that bathroom. I ended up in bed and that was the end of my cleaning. My husband did the rest. He did not allow me to do any cleaning anymore. I recovered, and then a few days later I started in with labor at 6 a.m., November 30th, 1957. By 1 p.m., the new baby was here. She was a wrinkly, hairless, pink little girl. Six pounds, thirteen ounces. I was overjoyed, even though I had behaved like a fool during the labor and delivery, since anything that happened below the waist was not discussed in my Catholic family. I vowed not to put my daughter in that kind of a compromised position, unaware of what her concerns should be, what to ask for, or what was even occurring, actually.

I wanted to nurse my baby. Lynn and I both considered it very important, although that was not the modern way in that era. Then there was a problem with the idea. The little thing would absolutely not cooperate. I kept on trying, to the point where the nurse began to discourage me. I insisted on talking to my doctor before I would give up. He urged me to begin bottle feeding with formula, since the baby was not getting anything out of the breastfeeding and was losing weight. Sadly, and with feelings of defeat, I accepted his advice and followed it.

Coming home from the hospital was quite the experience. My husband was concerned that I might spend all my time with the baby and not have time for him. The first two days he kept his distance from the new arrival. Then he jokingly called her face a wrinkled tomato, which hurt my feelings.

On the third day I saw him quietly slip into her room and he was in there awhile, so I snuck up to the door to see what was going on. He was by our baby Leslie's bed, looking down at her with a big grin on his face. He was playing with her hands. I was so relieved.

In mid-December of 1957, my husband took a trip to Las Cruces, New Mexico to see if he could get a job in the extension service, a government program working in agriculture on the county level. Lynn's bachelor's degree was in agriculture, and he had worked with them before he had joined the Air Force. He was hoping that if they had a place for him, it would be easier to slowly leave government service altogether. He wasn't sure what he wanted to do, but we both had decided the military was not for us, and we longed to live a civilian life.

He was gone for four days. I was in a new country, with a new baby in a strange town. He left behind names of people on the base that I could call if I needed anything, since we didn't even know our neighbors yet. Everything went fine, and he came back with positive news. Now we could leave the Air Force as we had planned.

Christmas of that year was a quiet event. We celebrated it with our new arrival, whom we had named Leslie, after the actress Leslie Caron, since we thought she was conceived the night we saw "Daddy Long Legs". We had a tree and packages of presents from both sets of parents. I enjoyed my mother-in-law's fruitcake immensely. It was so delicious I got the recipe and make it every year for Christmas. We rang in the New Year of 1958 equally quietly, not feeling the need, nor having the energy for anything more.

My husband applied for his discharge from the Air Force to be effective in early February.

He was raked over the coals by his superiors who wanted him to stay in, but he was determined to get out. He finally succeeded and in early February we packed up and moved from Salina, Kansas to Carlsbad, New Mexico, where a county agent's job was waiting for him.

We rented a house beside the railroad tracks which concerned me because of the baby, but she seemed to be lulled to sleep by the sound of the train.

New Mexico's warm weather was a sharp contrast to the ice and snow we had just left, and we enjoyed all the sunshine. We met a lawyer's widow who was a linguist, studying and teaching foreign languages in her home for a nominal fee. She volunteered to start me out in Spanish, which Lynn had learned in high school, but to which I had never been exposed. Foreign languages being my bag, I became very interested in my assignments and soon was better than my husband.

Chapter 7 | Love, Marriage and America

In spring, Lynn was supposed to go to a one week workshop on a Dude Ranch in Jemez Springs, New Mexico. He wanted me to come along. He called his parents and asked if his mother would come and take care of Leslie. The answer was yes, and my in-laws arrived a few weeks later. I was very nervous knowing that my housekeeping and cooking (which was undeveloped at the time) would be investigated and judged by Lynn's mother. I really liked my father-in-law and knew he would never judge anyone negatively without good reason. He was a great gentleman, always seeing the positive in everything and always being polite and kind.

We went to Jemez Springs, driving through mountains and Indian villages. The grounds of the Dude Ranch were beautiful, with lovely cabins arranged around a large courtyard. In addition to the individual cabins and dining facilities, there was a large hall for all sorts of activities. The furniture was rustic, as were the lamps and rugs and wall hangings. The fireplaces rendered coziness. The nights and mornings were quite cold up in the mountains.

I mingled with male and female county agents, I listened to discussions and I was invited to give a talk on German public schools, which I accepted. It was a challenge to speak before a large gathering in English. I wanted to fit in, and I also wanted to share my knowledge, but I was shaking inside through the whole thing. I got a good response and lots of questions, so I was quite proud of myself.

I did have an experience there however, which I was not so proud of.

The activities that were presented to the group were quite varied. One of them was square dancing. I had never seen square dancing in my life. There are dances in Germany that have some similarities, so I was confident and eager to learn, and I started out doing well. As the steps became more complicated I began to have trouble, and I threw a tantrum, stomping off the floor in tears, to the surprise of the people in my group. I had always been such a good dancer in Germany, so I was particularly frustrated not being able to square dance as smoothly as everyone else. Of course, they had all done it before, but I was impatient with myself and my pride was wounded. The whole thing

Tishi   REFUGEE • IMMIGRANT • MOTHER

was embarrassing.

The rest of the week was fun and flew by, and before we knew it we were on the drive home, although we took a quick detour to stop by the White Sands. The White Sands of New Mexico could not cease to amaze me. Miles of silky white sand spread out for us to play in. My husband and I were like two silly kids in a giant sand box. It was like a dream.

Arriving at home, I found Lynn's mother had taken good care of the house and the baby, and was much kinder than I had anticipated. In fact, her only complaint was concern that Leslie was not eating well, which I explained to her was something I had already talked to the doctor about. She was a healthy baby, she just didn't have a big appetite. His mother seemed satisfied and my in-laws stayed on for a few more rather pleasant days, and then they headed home.

At the end of May, we were contacted by my husband's main office in Las Cruses about a transfer to Clovis, New Mexico. My husband was not happy about that turn of events. He went ahead and rented us a house. He found one for a reasonable price that was fully furnished, which was what we needed. We always rented furnished houses since we were always on the move.

Unfortunately, he had not realized how terribly dirty this one was, and because of the price, no one was going to clean it but us. We had stuffed all our belongings into our little moving trailer, and arrived at a house we barely could stand to move into. I was pregnant again and unluckily for Lynn, the dirt and the smell of Clovis made me sick to my stomach. Clovis was a cattle town and when the wind blew the wrong direction, just trying to breath made one's eyes water. It made me nauseous. I was depressed and unable to help clean. My dear husband did it all. I could only take care of the baby and throw up. Those were my activities. Lynn did the rest.

Both of us did not like Clovis, New Mexico. The smell from the stockyards was awful. It was a small town with small minded people. It had at least thirty different churches and a lot of puritanical thinkers, not exactly my cup of tea. I was thoroughly unhappy there. I was so unhappy that I turned against my husband at times, threatening to pack

Chapter 7 | Love, Marriage and America

up and return to Germany, telling him that the entire town and he too, seemed like something out of a weird story.

Poor Lynn was not faring well there himself. It turned out his boss was a nasty demagogue named Phil, and the central office in Las Cruces had a hard time keeping that position filled. Agent after agent left the job because no one could stand to work for evil Phil. My good old husband hung in there and took care of our little family.

My pregnancy seemed to progress well, and our little one gave us much pleasure. She was an extremely active and rapidly developing baby. She was interested in everything and at a very young age, showed a charming and at times determined personality. She was also a big ham. We were delighted with her and had lots of fun. The only thing we worried about was her poor appetite. She remained skinny for her height until her early teens, when she finally filled out a bit. She is still slender, a trait which runs on my husband's side of the family.

Tishi   REFUGEE • IMMIGRANT • MOTHER

Tishi dancing at her "big white wedding"

Lynn and Tishi's wedding day

Tishi's passport

Tishi in Italy on honeymoon

Right: Tishi Sept. 1957 touring New York City

Chapter 7 | Love, Marriage and America

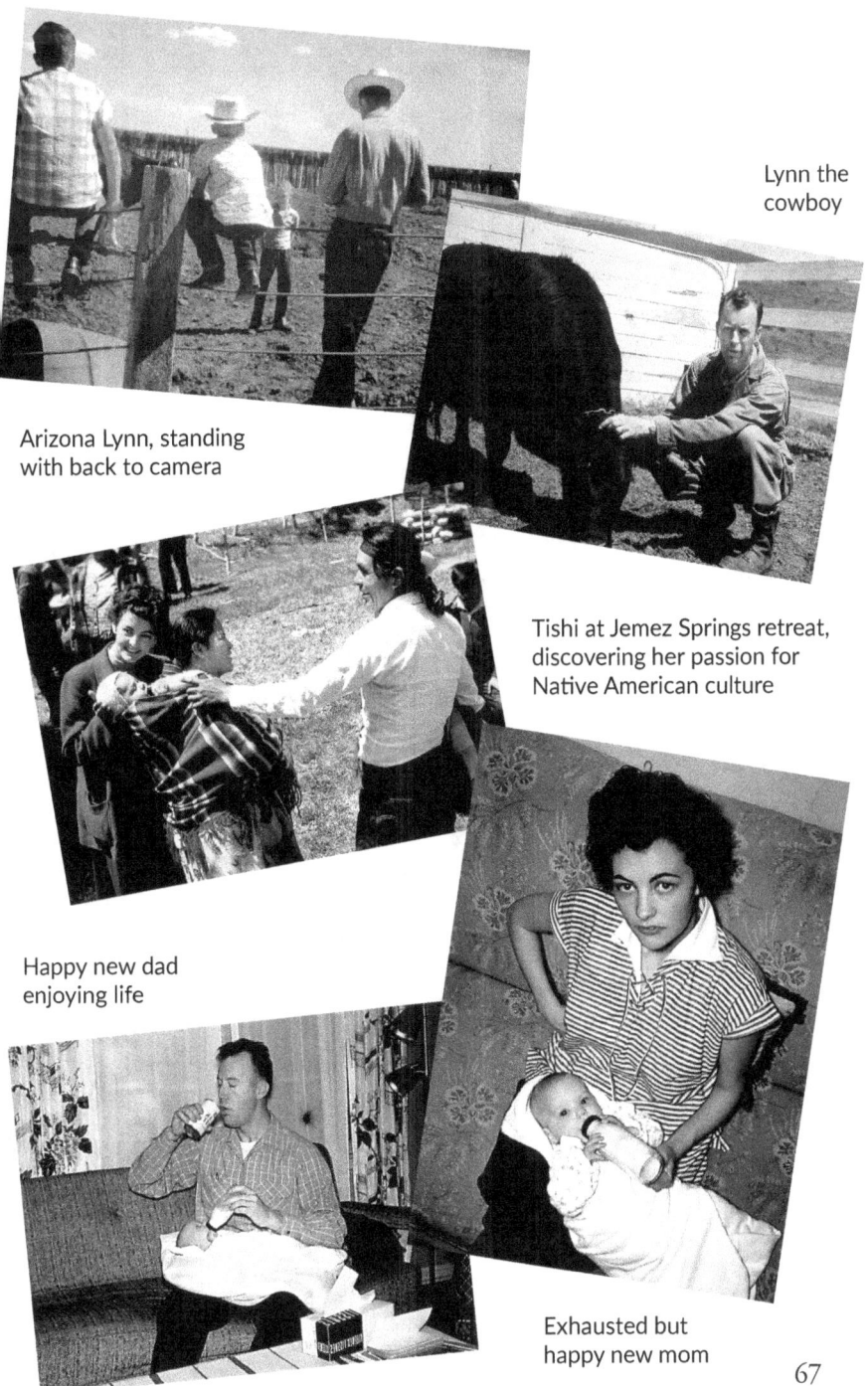

Lynn the cowboy

Arizona Lynn, standing with back to camera

Tishi at Jemez Springs retreat, discovering her passion for Native American culture

Happy new dad enjoying life

Exhausted but happy new mom

Tishi   REFUGEE • IMMIGRANT • MOTHER

Chapter 8
Heartbreak

In January 1959 I was supposed to have the new baby. My in-laws came this time to help us out. We all waited. No baby. After I was two weeks overdue, my physician, a general practitioner, told me I could mix a bottle of castor oil with orange juice and the concoction would probably start my labor. I did not want to do it. I waited one more week and then finally took his advice. Labor set in quite rapidly, and within four to five hours the baby arrived. After the delivery, when I wanted to see our new little girl I was told she had to be in an incubator since she was still spitting up mucus. I saw her, she was beautiful, and with dark hair, like mine. We named her Carina, after a night star. At first everyone acted like the mucus problem would just pass, but as days passed and it didn't, I became frantic. My physician finally became concerned about her condition. It took five days to make the diagnosis: esophageal-tracheal fistula. She was rushed to Lubbock, Texas, to a hospital with more sophisticated facilities where a specialist was going to operate on her. Lynn and my father-in-law followed behind the ambulance to Lubbock, my husband later describing to me how our new daughter looked him directly in the eyes at the Lubbock hospital, where the specialist refused to operate, stating that she was too weak to survive the operation. She did not survive the night. Lynn and his father came back with the sad report. Lynn was completely broken up about it.

I was in shock. After nine months of caring, and worrying and loving and caring, nothing...nothing.

Tishi   REFUGEE • IMMIGRANT • MOTHER

I felt like this could not be true, this could not be my life, this could not be me, this could not be happening. I had lived through horrors as a child, but nothing felt quite as horrifying as this. It felt like a nightmare. My in-laws left, there was no baby for them to help with. In hindsight, I realize that my mother-in-law could not take it, having lost a toddler herself to meningitis. My husband and I went to bury our baby, leaving our firstborn with a neighbor for a short period of time. We buried her ourselves, in a small cemetery outside Clovis, driving back in a heavy sandstorm. It was so sad.

I tried not to be overpowered by my grief and told myself it was probably for the best. Had baby Carina made it, the specialist had told my husband, she would most likely have dealt with severe stomach troubles her whole life. After some time I decided to turn toward the living and embraced my little girl Leslie with all my heart. I wanted to take the best care of her that I could, and I did. (I think).

Chapter 9

Picking Up and Going On

In the spring of 1959 the divorcée, whose house we had rented, wanted to move back into it. We looked for another house and found one closer to town. After we moved in, Lynn had to go to Las Cruces for two to three days of lectures at New Mexico State University, as part of his job. He came back convinced he wanted to return to college and finish his master's degree.

Even though it meant moving yet again, I was delighted. Back to school, on a college campus.

That meant interesting lectures for me too!

In September we packed up and headed north to Washington State University in Pullman, Washington. The town was practically dead, only 9000 people. But the university was interesting.

At first we lived in student housing. Later, we moved into a duplex, where my husband handled the janitorial duties for the one house, and another two duplexes up the street. This way we could live at reduced rent. His tuition came from the GI Bill. We managed.

Meanwhile it had become 1960.

We had some pleasant neighbors across the street who were naturalized Egyptians, meaning they had become U.S. citizens, something I was thinking about doing also. He was a professor in horticulture at the university, and she was a lovely and vivacious woman. Our children played together regularly and they were astounded at our bright little girl. We had a professor living next door to us too. That family had older children and a dog. The eldest babysat for us often and our little one visited with them two or three times a week. To their amazement, she put puzzles for six year olds together at three years old, without any problem. Everyone also remarked on her vocabulary and her perfect pronunciation. She spoke both German and English. We were thrilled with our offspring.

My husband Lynn had trouble at first adjusting to college, but after a while it became routine and he enjoyed his new life. His thesis for his master's degree was coming along. By June, 1960 he had finished his master's degree. I had typed his thesis with a lot of moaning and groaning.

Our relationship seemed strained at times because he was so busy with his studies and taking care of three houses, while I was tutoring four hours of German a day, preparing Ph.D. candidates for their foreign language exams. There was no time left for us to be alone and seek each other's companionship. When I fell into bed, tired out from the day, I was not interested in sexual relations, since I cannot make love strictly on a physical basis. I have to know that I am loved and not just being used for sex. We started to argue about our sex life, which we had done only once before, back in Carlsbad, New Mexico. My husband could not understand how I could have such thoughts, considering we were married and committed to one another and our family. He could not see how I could feel used when he clearly loved me. He argued that sex was a physical release and if we were too tired for much else, there was nothing wrong with just having that release. Our fight escalated to the point where he slapped me once, as he had done that one time in New Mexico too. The result was that I cried and he felt like a louse. He never slapped me again. When we made up, I confessed that I realized I was reliving my first sexual experience with Francois in Munich. Things took a turn for the better when I admitted that. I was absolutely scared of pure sex and have this phobia even now sometimes.

In the winter of 1960-61, I found myself pregnant again, but I noticed a lot of spotting. I went to the doctor, who wanted to put me on some form of progesterone or progestin to hold the baby in. I argued that if there was something wrong with the pregnancy, I would

Chapter 9 | Picking Up and Going On

like whatever is wrong to come out now and not nine months later. I could not go through that again. I did not want a "patched up" pregnancy and refused to take the pills, for which I was glad. When I was in my third month, something called a fleshy mole came out of me, and it was an awful experience. I had been hemorrhaging and was in bed at home. The doctor came to the house in the morning and said I would probably miscarry. Later on my husband came home between classes. I went to the bathroom and felt something big coming out of me. I felt like I was fainting, let out a yell and fell on the floor. Lynn came in and took care of me. He saved the fleshy thing for my doctor. The doctor came back to the house and gave me antibiotics and prescribed bed rest. The fleshy mole was deemed to be a pregnancy that never really developed.

One of my friends had female problems and had gone to a gynecologist in Spokane and told him what happened to me. He felt I needed to be checked out and blood tests ought to be run on me for one year. I decided to go see him since I had only been seeing a general practitioner in Pullman. The Spokane doctor actually provided relief. It turned out that I was fine and within the normal percentage of pregnancies that don't come to fruition. However, I was quite put off by the idea of having babies after my last two experiences, and wasn't sure if I ever wanted to try again. My husband Lynn was quite understanding.

On May 1, 1961, I became a naturalized citizen of the United States of America. I had studied the Constitution and felt quite accomplished with this achievement. It was a much needed shining moment.

Life continued moving along nicely when Lynn began having problems with his major professor, a Cambridge graduate. Lynn had acquired an assistantship, doing research in bio-chem, which was quite a coup. The professor put people on my husband's committee that were important to him, that were involved in his career, but not conducive to my husband's studies and assignments. There were two professors that we both objected to. I told Lynn, "Don't let him do this to you," but Lynn felt trapped because his major professor was in control of the assistantship and could withdraw it at any time. I pointed out to my husband that one of these guys would try to do him in, since they both had a reputation for it. I felt that Lynn's course of non-action was career suicide. After some time it did become obvious, even to my optimistic husband, that there was a personality clash between him and this one man who thought himself the god of Washington State University. I gently advised that we move to another school, and after a lot of soul searching, and establishing connections with Oregon State, we pulled out of Pullman and headed for Corvallis, Oregon in July 1962.

Meanwhile, our closest friends in Pullman, the Egyptian neighbors with whom we argued about the existence of Israel, but otherwise had good relations with, moved to Indonesia. They had been offered a job with AID, an international assistance program under President Kennedy. They relocated to Jakarta.

Nothing was keeping us in Pullman and we welcomed the change to Oregon. Corvallis was a lovely, warm and fertile town. With the high humidity, the shrubs, flowers and vegetables all grew in abundance. There were all sorts of exotic looking trees and foliage we had never seen before. Our daughter Leslie took to calling a certain genus of tree whose "leaves" were dark green and looked to her like monkey tails, "the monkey trees". The winters were mild, though rainy, compared to Pullman's beautiful snow. I liked the campus, and was looking forward to all sorts of open lectures like those I had attended at Washington State.

We enrolled Leslie in kindergarten. Lynn set up his research program immediately and got right to work. I advertised to graduate students for German tutoring, which, after a slow start the first six months, I then had plenty of.

In late September of 1962, we received word that my father-in-law had died. We drove to the funeral in Douglas, barely making it with auto trouble along the way. He had been 80, and died of a heart attack while fixing something on the roof. We were not prepared for this because as far as we knew, he was well and healthy, still climbing on the roof to fix things! The suddenness was shocking. After the funeral we had to go back rather quickly, because my husband had all his work waiting at home. The drive home was somber. I knew we would miss this wonderful, gentle, kind and loving man. We invited Lynn's mother to come and visit us after things calmed down.

My husband was happy with his professors and he liked the men

Chapter 9 | Picking Up and Going On

on his committee. Everything seemed trouble free. It was an enjoyable time, even if it was a little rough financially. We had taken out government loans which had to be paid off ten years after finishing college. I had the income from my tutoring, and my dad sent us small contributions. My mother-in-law had done so until now, but we told her no more, now that Lynn's dad was gone. We figured she could use the money. Lynn took a job as a night watchman in a saw mill, making rounds, rain or not. We also took Leslie, along with another young, fun struggling family we met, and picked crops, mostly green beans and rhubarb. The kids worked, but also ran around in the fields, and weeks later we showed Leslie canned rhubarb and green beans in the grocery store, and told her those could be the very ones she had picked. That seemed to fascinate her. For years after that, she wondered aloud if they were, whenever she saw a can of green beans. These were hard, but also extremely pleasant, times. We celebrated by going to the beach, forty miles away, but a treat every time.

Almost a year later, in the fall of 1963, my mother-in-law finally took us up on our offer to visit. However, she brought her two sisters along for the visit in our small apartment. I was appalled. I had not expected an entire expedition when I had invited her, and had no idea how to accommodate them. Short of funds and space, we made do, and made the best of it.

I had a little trouble coping with the three elder females, who felt they knew my husband best, and what was best, period. Aunt Jewel, the sweet one, was easy. But the other two definitely threw their might around, and I felt overpowered. Once the two aunts left, we just had Lynn's mother with us...and that went okay. It was actually probably a better experience than if my own mother had been there. Most of the time my mother-in-law tried to be agreeable, but there were times when she would slip, and turn downright offensive. I think she just never could get over the fact that I was a foreigner. At the same time, my own mother had been writing me advice on how to dress Leslie, what to wear myself, and basically how I should live.

I found a way to appease both of them. My mother-in-law loved to sew, and my mother sent patterns of dresses Leslie should be wearing,

Tishi   REFUGEE • IMMIGRANT • MOTHER

according to her. So I had Eunice, Lynn's mother, sew dresses from those patterns, which I took photos of, and mailed to my mother. Everything was peaceful. Both mothers felt proud and Leslie had new clothes. I felt pretty tricky coming up with that.

I could not come up with a way to keep Eunice out of my kitchen though. At first it was nice to have some help. Then I felt thoroughly pushed out of control in my own home. The second I set foot in the kitchen to start dinner, she showed up, sniffing around and frowning, while inquiring what I was making and how I was doing it. When I told her, she always proceeded to take over and make the dinner. I did not know how to handle this, after all, she "only wanted to help", and make sure her baby boy got his dinner prepared the way she did it at home.

The month long visit went by, and I got busy typing the rough drafts for Lynn's thesis again. This thesis was for his Ph.D., and this time, I was not going to be typing out the final copy as well. Things were coming along smoothly. The kindergarten teacher was raving about our unusually talented, mature and lovely daughter, which made us very happy. The prelims went well, as did finalizing Lynn's thesis. Aside from the terrible news that our President John F. Kennedy was assassinated, our lives were coming along quite well. In January 1964 my husband took his last final exams without any trouble and we were done. Lynn had his doctorate, and a research position waiting for him at Cornell University, which we were looking forward to with great expectations.

We took a long, cold, snowy drive through Canada to visit some college friends of Lynn's on our way to New York. We drove over frozen lakes, saw a professional hockey game and went to an almost frozen Niagara Falls. Ithaca, New York was also thick with ice and snow when we arrived there. We rented a small, two story, three bedroom house. We had acquired some furniture in Pullman and had sent it ahead with Mayflower. The movers did not arrive for two weeks. We decided never to use that moving company again.

Chapter 9 | Picking Up and Going On

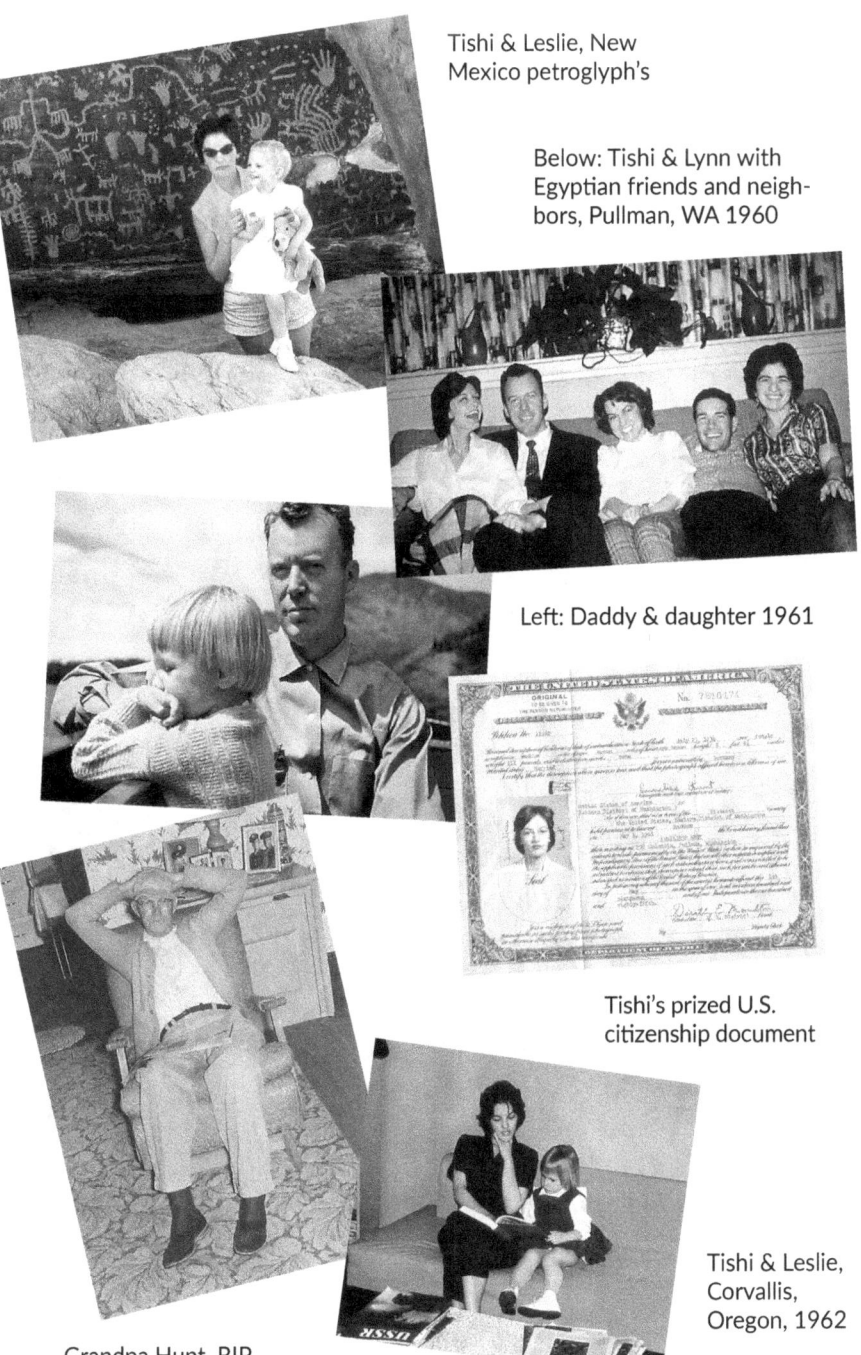

Tishi & Leslie, New Mexico petroglyph's

Below: Tishi & Lynn with Egyptian friends and neighbors, Pullman, WA 1960

Left: Daddy & daughter 1961

Tishi's prized U.S. citizenship document

Grandpa Hunt, RIP

Tishi & Leslie, Corvallis, Oregon, 1962

Tishi   REFUGEE • IMMIGRANT • MOTHER

Chapter 10
Ithaca, New York

The people in the east were not as friendly as out west. The neighbors would not lend me their vacuum cleaner while I waited for mine. This was quite a cold response in comparison to what I had become accustomed to in America. I just wanted to get the house cleaned up. I felt strange among these kind of people and it required some adjustment.

Our belongings arrived, and we had to buy a little more furniture, and finally got settled in. The house was simple and old, but relatively nice. I resented that we had not gotten a place near the university, so I could run to some lectures by myself during the day. There were no inexpensive houses near campus, only apartments. Lynn thought it was more important, especially with a child, to have a yard and the privacy of a house, rather than be close to the campus. We only had one car, and I didn't even know how to drive, so I was extremely resentful regarding this. I disagreed with my husband, pointing out that being closer would serve two purposes. It would cut down on his commute, and I could have walked there during the day.

I also thought that being near all that activity would be stimulating for Leslie. There were parks around the campus too. But Lynn had the final word. And I felt locked up with my household duties.

In the spring of 1964 I was pregnant again. After the sadness and problems, I was ready to try again, so we planned for this, and it happened immediately. I was so sick with this pregnancy I had to sleep with a bucket beside me. After three months, the throwing up finally stopped and I had better days ahead of me.

There were a lot of German post-doctorates at Cornell University, and after being so long out of touch with anything German, I was hesitant about dealing with German arrogance. They were mostly young families like us, with fathers who studied here in the U.S., but they intended to return to Germany. My husband connected with a few of them in his department, thinking I would be excited, not realizing how nervous I was that I was going to be considered a deserter, since I had no intentions of moving back. We were invited to a party with so many Germans I was amazed. I met the whole group. Things went far better than I had anticipated, but I spotted the typical Germans on their soapboxes right away, one in particular. His style of arguing reminded me of my father, talking over everyone and making sure his, and only his points were heard above the rest.

I became well acquainted with his wife later on, since we both had our babies close together. She admitted to me that whenever he had a discussion about anything, he usually handled it like warfare. He did not engage in discussions to learn or share information, strictly to assert himself. I found him boorish, but after some time I accepted him for what he was and our families remained friends for years.

In August of that year, my father came for a visit from Germany. It had been almost seven years since I had seen him. I had retained a lot of my old grudges, and when the plane landed at Kennedy Airport, I was not sure of my feelings. When I saw my father, a mixture of joy and irritation overcame me. He was delighted that we had come to pick him up, and also, that he had a lovely grandchild waiting for him that could speak German fluently. His happiness disarmed me. I couldn't even remember what specifically I had resentments about. My parents' bickering? Isn't that part of marriage? Granted, they could have handled things better, but given the stress of the war and how he got his family through it and thrived once more? Was I still angry because he didn't accept Lynn at first? He was the first to come around. And what father wants his daughter to marry someone and move to the other side of the world?

We drove back to Ithaca, arriving home in the middle of the night.

Chapter 10 | Ithaca, New York

Leslie found it exciting. And my dad got oriented and accustomed to our routine quickly. We had a great time with him. He loved going to the bank and having Leslie be his interpreter. We went on several outings, picnics, and a trip to Washington D.C. In spite of my pregnancy, I still had a wonderful time in Washington. We saw all the sights and experienced the city as the center of the U.S. government. We traveled back to Ithaca and on to more sightseeing in upstate New York with its rolling hills, waterfalls and gorges. Three weeks were over in no time and it was time for my father to leave. We all stood there at Kennedy airport with tears in our eyes, it had been so much fun. No one wanted it to be over.

Early in December, after breakfast one morning, my husband Lynn told me that he had received a call from my father at the University, telling him that my mother had died of a heart attack on November 29. My father did not know how to break the news to me personally, so he had decided to contact Lynn at work. They were both worried about how I would react, especially considering that I was about to give birth.

I was shocked. I could not believe it. We had just received a long letter from her the previous week. I felt like my world was falling apart. I became so concerned about the baby though, that I told myself I could not let her death upset me too much, and I would have to deal with it later. I did not want any complications so close to the time of delivery. I was not going to let anything interfere with me having a healthy and happy baby. From my previous experiences, I was afraid that something might go wrong again so I blocked all sadness out of my mind.

I wrote my dad to that effect since, once the news was out, he seemed to want to feed me all the details, and I did not want to hear about them. I explained my situation and my feelings to him. He said he understood, but I knew I had hurt him. He needed to unload on someone, and my sister was not particularly receptive either, I learned later.

On a snowy December 19, 1964, our son Mark was born and pronounced a healthy baby boy. It was a beautiful birth that I treasured because, as big as he was, (8lbs. 6 oz.), I was able to watch everything in a mirror. He was a huge baby for a small person like me, but it was an amazing and wonderful experience in an excellent hospital. We were all overjoyed. Leslie was happy because she was the only one in her class that did not have any brothers or sisters at home. One brother saved her from what she considered a low status state.

My friendships with the German wives of University colleagues of Lynn's blossomed. We visited each other often and sometimes had coffee together and once in awhile, a party.

By the summer of 1965, we decided it was time to go out west and introduce our latest addition to the family. I dreaded the trip with a baby, but my husband wanted his mother to see Mark. Mark was a gigantic baby in contrast to Leslie. I figured he had his genes from Lynn, since my side of the family was relatively small. We were not the tall, blond Germans people think of. We were small to medium, some light and some dark, of southern German and Austrian heritage. Lynn's tall, blond family, although of English/Irish ancestry, actually had more of that Nordic look. I could just imagine how Grandma would react to seeing Mark, being reminded of her own big baby boys. I used to get constipated and get headaches around her, but I understood, said OK, and off we drove to Arizona.

It was a hot trip in August, but I was right, Grandma was beside herself with joy. She was the most hospitable and warm she had ever been with me. We visited with friends and relatives in Douglas, then drove to Phoenix to see my husband's brother Lee and his family. On the way to Douglas we had stopped in Tucumcari, New Mexico, to see Lynn's other brother Norman.

Norman was divorced and drank too much, but was honored that we visited. All in all, the trip was a big success. It also was the last time I saw my mother-in-law.

We returned home and resumed our life. We were starting to think about a more permanent job situation for Lynn. We decided we wanted to accept a position only at a university. Industry was out. Jobs in Lynn's field of biological research that were not through universities lacked integrity. However, university jobs did not pay as well, we soon found out. There were several possibilities, but we did not like the pay. It did not seem suitable for raising a family. Half jokingly, my husband told me about a position that the corporate pharmaceutical company G.D.

Chapter 10 | Ithaca, New York

Searle had open. He wondered if he should go to the interview. I was aghast! He was talking about going against our beliefs, into industry? I told him no, never. He said the pay was at least eight to ten thousand dollars more a year than any university position. I agreed we could look into it, but not take it seriously. The next thing I knew, he had an appointment for an interview. It was the spring of 1966. Before he left, we both agreed we were not really considering it, although why we both thought he should go, I don't know.

Lynn flew to Chicago and had his meeting in Skokie, Illinois, a nearby suburb. When he returned home, he was greatly enthused with his interview, and with G.D. Searle, the company. The position was in basic research and paid far better than we had even thought. He also liked the working conditions, which included having his own lab. He was also assured freedom in his research. These were precisely the things he wanted. I myself, was not as enthusiastic. I had become accustomed to university life, and could not imagine living without it. I hated the idea of not being in a university town. Chicago and it's suburban sprawl did not interest me at all. I was happy for Lynn, that he would have such an opportunity, but I felt it came with a price. He would be researching the safety of pharmaceutical products that were part of the corporate machine.

We discussed it and discussed it. The money was seductive. The job offer came. We accepted. We were both sort of surprised at ourselves that we had changed.

My mother-in-law was ill and was supposed to have an operation. She was in a hospital in Phoenix where brother Lee lived. Lynn went to see her, making a quick stop in Chicago first, to find a place for us to live. He rented a house in Northbrook, a nice suburb, calling me to describe it and tell me the price. I could not believe how much rent cost there. I finally gave my approval after he told me that apartments were close to the same amount, yet with a house, we would have a private driveway, garage and yard for the children.

He went on his way to Phoenix to see his mother and returned feeling good about her condition, as well as about renting the house. He described suburban living to me and I was not so sure I would like it.

83

Tishi REFUGEE • IMMIGRANT • MOTHER

Although it wasn't a university with lectures and activities, it was close to the second largest city in America, which meant culture, ballet, museums of all kinds, art, theater, and a lot of opportunity to explore. I decided to look at it as a new adventure.

Chapter 10 | Ithaca, New York

Tishi, Leslie, and Tishi's father, New York City, 1964

Below: Waiting in line to tour the White House, pregnant Tishi and another mother share a moment, 1964

Left: Lynn, Tishi and Leslie with German friends in Ithaca, 1965

Petite Tishi with her big healthy baby boy, 1965

Summer 1965 in Ithaca, happy Mom and daughter

Lynn in his research lab at Cornell University

Tishi   REFUGEE • IMMIGRANT • MOTHER

Chapter 11
Chicago 1966-1976

In late August 1966, we moved to Northbrook, Illinois. I liked the house. It was a modern, three bedroom, split-level with high ceilings, and a lot nicer than our house in Ithaca. Now I understood the price. The neighborhood was nice, with all sorts of different people, including a family with five children living right next door.

Lynn found his job and working situation to his satisfaction and remarked on the freedom he enjoyed in his research. My father sent me some money from my mother's inheritance, with which we were considering buying a house. We decided not to buy a house in Northbrook, because we thought we could afford an even nicer neighborhood. Lynn's Aunt Jewel had given him some cattle that we sold off bit by bit when we needed extra money. We chose to do that again and have a comfortable down-payment. We began looking for a house.

In December 1966 we celebrated our little man's second birthday. He earned that nickname because he walked very straight and erect with his little hands clasped behind him. He was adorable, but slow in his development in comparison to his sister. He was 16 months before he could walk, although he was chubby and had a lot of weight to support. Unlike Leslie, he had taken to breastfeeding like a champion, and he was an avid eater, at least until I introduced him to junior baby food. He did not like all that lumpy stuff. He also refused to drink from a cup for quite awhile. At two years of age he only said words, not sentences, and not many at that. It was a total reversal from our firstborn. I felt frustrated at times. I tried to stimulate him in all sorts of ways. I invited neighborhood children his own age over, with their mothers, but he did not socialize with them. He went off and played by himself. That was the hardest thing for me to understand. His sister always had been in the center of every group she associated with. He was a loner. I kept inviting different children to play, hoping the situation would change, but it did not, for a long while.

In the spring of 1967, we bought a house in the nice suburb of Glenview. It was another three bedroom, split level, but with bigger rooms, a bigger yard, a two car garage and a longer driveway. It was in poor condition because the owners had not taken care of it. They had been too busy getting a divorce. We thought it was a great deal and this way we could fix it up gradually, and to our liking. So we started to work on it ourselves, before we even moved in. We removed wallpaper and wood paneling and painted as many rooms as we could before our move in date. In the midst of all these preparations Grandma, my mother-in-law, died. She had become quite senile in the past year, not remembering things from one day to the next. We had gotten her a nurse, who lived with her, and whom she dismissed, asserting she had stolen a ring from her. She had been in the hospital for some tests and insisted on getting out of bed when the hospital nurse told her she needed to rest. She refused, stood up, fell over, hit her head, and now she was dead. She was 76 years old.

Lynn flew alone to the funeral. A friend of his kept helping me with the work in the new house. We had to be out of the Northbrook house by a definite date, so we were, so-to-speak, between houses. When my husband returned he dove full force into the work, partially to get it done quickly, and partially because he could immerse himself into an activity and forget his sadness. In July, 1967, we moved in, but there was a lot left to do. It would take years...

For me, it was the first home I lived in that was not rented but owned, since we had left Czechoslovakia. My parents were just building a big beautiful house when we left Germany, but I had only seen pictures. This house in Glenview was a very important thing for me. We continued to work on it as much as possible. By Christmas I was

Chapter 11 | Chicago 1966-1976

thoroughly constipated and felt quite miserable from all the tension and stress I put myself through.

I picked Dr. Etheridge out of the phone book and got an appointment. He only shook his head when I told him how I got myself into such a situation. He put me on Probanthine to loosen my bowels and Phenobarbital for anxiety. I was on them for four months and then my problems cleared up.

Meanwhile I was getting more concerned about my little fellow. He was now three years old and spoke only in words. He still played basically by himself. I put him under too much pressure, trying to speak properly with him all the time, and trying to get him to practice his pronunciation. Lynn explained that it was a developmental condition and that he too, had been extremely slow with his speech development. He asked me to just be patient, but it was difficult after the fast development of our first one. I had to learn to not compare the children. At times, when all four of us drove somewhere in the car and Leslie would just talk and talk and talk and Mark would just sit silently with us, I felt so sorry for him having this big sister (7 years older) carrying all the conversation. I tried to include him, even making her be quiet and focusing my attention only on him, but after her torrent of words he was usually speechless.

We intended to go to Germany in the summer of 1968, the first time since I had come to this country in 1957. I knew many things had changed at home and that I was in for a culture shock. I would go to a house I had never lived in, my mother was gone, and I had to get to know my new stepmother. From all the letters and phone calls, she seemed to be a nice person, but it was sure to be awkward. Aside from my father, who had only seen Leslie, no one in my family, and extended family, of which there were many, had seen my children. And I knew Germany itself had changed, as well as people's lifestyles.

We went in July, 1968. It was quite the experience. Emotionally draining. I found I had difficulty expressing myself with ease in German. English now came more readily to my tongue and my friends and relatives joked that I spoke German with a bit of an American accent. I didn't really care all that much about it, but it was still disconcerting.

Tishi   REFUGEE • IMMIGRANT • MOTHER

My father had built an impressive four story house, so there was plenty of room for our whole family. My sensitive Mark woke up crying every night in this big, strange house, where people spoke a strange language. He had heard it a little at home, because Lynn and I still spoke with Leslie once in awhile. Mark had been so slow with English, I had not wanted to cause him any stress, so I had kept the German low key. But Leslie had kept up, and was able to converse with the whole family. One evening, after some wine, my sister laughingly announced in front of everyone that she liked my daughter, but not my son! What she mistook as rude, was just Mark being shy. Before we had left for Germany, I had complained to our pediatrician about Mark's slow verbal development. The doctor did not seem to be concerned, and told me to give the poor little fellow time. His motor skills and cognitive test results were all normal.

My stepmother was not a very chatty person. She seemed more accustomed to reacting than acting. At least that was my impression. We were both polite and nice to each other but did not really get to know one another. I went to visit some of my old friends. They had changed somewhat of course, but basically they were still the same.

Germany had drastically changed. Everybody seemed to be prosperous. There were almost as many cars as in the U.S. My dad drove a Mercedes, my sister had an Audi. It had taken time, but my family had achieved the status and comfort level I had been born into, before the war. Ulm, the city where I had gone to school after the war, which had been practically destroyed, was now booming. There were so many people and tourists shopping on just a regular afternoon, it seemed more crowded to me than our suburban mall back home outside Chicago. What a surprise!

Returning home, we tried to digest the trip. A miraculous thing had happened with Mark in Germany. Surrounded by all these German speaking people, including his bi-lingual sister, he started to speak English in complete sentences. Out of the blue, just like that. We were ecstatic. It was as if he felt so isolated that he made the supreme effort. He also shed the diapers. Day AND night. He was three years old and finally done! So the trip was definitely a good thing for him, as it

Chapter 11 | Chicago 1966-1976

turned out. I was so relieved and proud at how the improvement had happened.

Our house was a continuous project and I was looking forward to the day that the entire house would be intact. We had just finished remodeling the family room in the partial basement and we were thoroughly excited to gather and watch television or play ping pong.

In the winter of 1968-69, much to my surprise, I discovered I was pregnant again. I could not believe it was true. I was done with having babies. I had a boy and a girl. I practiced birth control. Either condoms or a diaphragm or both. There was no room in the house for a baby, it would change our entire life. There was a Down's Syndrome child in our neighborhood whose mother had been older when she had her. We also had family friends through Lynn's work who had a Down's Syndrome baby, also with a mother who gave birth past 35. No, I was not going to have another baby, there were too many risks involved, and there were no provisions in our home to accommodate another child. After those years of being crammed into a room with my whole family, I strongly believed every child should have their own room. Our house only had three bedrooms. I decided I was going to seek an abortion. If it had been four years later, I could have gotten one, after Roe Vs. Wade passed. However, it was 1969, I was 36 years old, and my gynecologist, Dr. Buckingham, blew his stack at the idea. He told me it was unethical.

"Perhaps this is done in some other country, but not this one. You are a healthy, married woman with a good provider for a husband," he said. He told me in no uncertain terms to forget about the idea. I went home and wanted to kill myself. After all the strife and struggle through all these years, I was worn out, I needed some rest. I had looked forward to relaxing after the house was done. Now I would have to start all over. I walked around as if in a daze, inconsolable. I did not want to have another baby and society was forcing me to, because of beliefs I did not even share. My mood changed back and forth between depression and anger.

Strangely enough, I did not have to vomit at all this time, in contrast to all three other pregnancies. I could not even believe I was preg-

91

nant, since at first there were no signs except for missed periods and the pregnancy test. I continued not to be nauseated at all, a symptom I had with every pregnancy. It was the easiest pregnancy of all four. I felt like this baby was giving me a break, which made me feel better about having it. I broke the news gently to Leslie, who was jubilant. Mark was a little more hesitant.

In accordance with my beliefs, we had to make some changes to the house in expectation of the new baby. I wanted the baby's room next to mine, which meant moving Leslie somewhere else. We decided to cut the family room downstairs in half, and one side was converted into a bedroom for Leslie. We added a bathroom because the laundry room was down there and the plumbing was already set up. She felt like she had her own suite. Bedroom, T.V. room, and her own little bathroom with a shower. The ping pong table had to go outside, which was fine in the summer. Leslie's old room became the new baby room and I was actually excited preparing it for the new baby. It was all working out quite nicely and we got lucky with the construction. It was reasonable and went smoothly. Lynn did quite a bit of it himself. Everything was ready before I went to the hospital for delivery.

I had labor all afternoon long on August 28th, 1969, but the contractions stayed the same length apart and didn't get stronger. I finally called Dr. Buckingham at 6 p.m. and he told me to go to the hospital. After I went through the process of being admitted, my contractions started coming closer together, but still were not strong enough to indicate that I was ready for delivery.

Halfway through the evening Dr. Buckingham showed up and gave me something to speed up the contractions. I reminded him I wanted natural childbirth, no medication, that's how I had all my deliveries and I felt like a pro about it. He tried to convince me to have the spinal block but I refused. I said I would only take the shot in the thigh right before the baby comes out. He came back three more times trying to talk me into the spinal. The third time I was struggling a bit with the pain and finally gave in. I thought if it was that important to him I would be better off following the procedure he was obviously accustomed to. I resented however, not doing my own thing and felt

Chapter 11 | Chicago 1966-1976

somehow cheated.

The delivery was the easiest ever. It was a perfect girl. Whether I inserted my diaphragm incorrectly or however it happened, I would refer to her as the best mistake I ever made. For all my misgivings about having another baby, she was as easy as a baby can be. In the recovery room my husband and I marveled at what an unusually pretty face she had for a newborn. She really was a very pretty baby. Of course the best thing was that she was also perfectly healthy. Everything had progressed so smoothly with this one, our main consideration was that it would continue to, and it did. She was a dream baby.

I had been watching "Romper Room" with Mark, who was four, at the end of my pregnancy. They always looked into a mirror at the end of the show and mentioned children's names, sending them greetings. That is where I heard the name Karleen and immediately loved it. I knew if I had a girl, that is what I would name her. It sounded a little like Carina, so I was honoring her, but it was a different name, so this baby would have her own identity. Funny thing, she looked a little like Carina. And she was healthy.

When I brought her home from the hospital we noticed Mark seemed to have a case of sibling rivalry. He had a constant worried look on his face for the first few days Karleen was home. Leslie, on the other hand, was delighted to have this living baby doll to play with. After awhile, I let Leslie, who was eleven years old, change Karleen's diapers. After a few weeks I let her feed Karleen the bottle. Leslie was thrilled.

Mark was not thrilled. At four years old, he looked at his little sister as an intruder. We made a point not to neglect him, giving him extra attention. It worked, and he soon became accustomed to having this little thing around. I was 36 and Lynn was almost 42. Having a baby at our age slowed us down of course, but having a built-in babysitter was a great help.

****

Tishi   REFUGEE • IMMIGRANT • MOTHER

Clockwise from top: Mark & Leslie, Northbrook, Illinois, Xmas 1966; Tishi's father building his 4-story house in Germany, 1960; Leslie & Tishi in the corner at the Plassenburg Castle where Tishi lived for six months as a refugee, 1968; Family photo in Germany, 1968; Family shopping in boom-town Ulm,1968; Pretty Baby Karleen, 1970; Karleen, Leslie's living doll, Easter 1970

Chapter 11 | Chicago 1966-1976

In the summer of 1970, when Karleen was a year old, my husband's brother Lee, his wife Shirley, and their two sons came to visit. Later on that summer, their eldest daughter Terry came with her family, and the following spring, Lee's other daughter Jeannie came to stay for a few days. It was a busy year for visitors from my husband's side of the family. It was a lot of work, since at the same time I was hosting house-guests, the baby needed a lot of attention. It was also a lot of fun though, because I personally always enjoy Lee and his family. In contrast to us, they are the most soft-spoken people, very gentle and quiet; we are a lot more noisy. The only unpleasant visitor we had that year was Lynn's other brother Norman. Norman drank too much and insisted on rearranging the household to suit his needs. He could never adjust or adapt.

Our son Mark started kindergarten that year. I was apprehensive about it because he was so shy and introverted, and I felt uncertain as to whether he could handle real school yet. He had finally started to play with other children at about three and a half years old. We considered this great progress. He was definitely a late bloomer. He did everything he was supposed to do, but just a little later than other children. It often made me anxious and impatient with him, and he felt that pressure from me. In 1970, as he started kindergarten, I insisted that he be tested on speech and vocabulary because I felt he needed help. At that time, the Glenview schools did not start any speech programs until first grade. They agreed to my request. He was tested and found to be in need of the service, and he received it. I enrolled him in the summer speech program and took him there three times a week. His speech improved, and by the time first grade started, I was satisfied that he could keep up and join in. He just had needed a little nudge.

In 1972, I had another bout with digestive problems. I went back to Dr. Etheridge, who diagnosed the same problem I had before: my intestines were stopped up. To make sure there was nothing else, he had upper and lower GI tests run, and aside from some pesky gallstones, which he assumed I had developed from poor nutrition during and after the war, everything came back negative. I promised him one day I would have the gallstones removed, but surgery was not something I wanted to deal with at a time when I still had a toddler. The gallstones were not the problem. The reason I was upset enough to cause blockage, was that my husband was having difficulties with his boss, who was a former colleague. The man had suddenly been promoted two, then three steps upward, and was drunk with power. My husband clashed sharply with him and finally realized the fellow would get rid of him if he actually could, but so far, all they had was a difference of opinion. I did not want it to escalate, and have Lynn get fired for something that was actually trivial. The situation bothered me terribly. The insecurity, plus Lynn's unhappiness about it, seemed to overpower me at times. I took the medication and everything cleared up, digestive-wise. I told Lynn to cool it, and to just hold on for the moment. I told him to keep an eye and ear out for an opening somewhere else, and if there was an opening, to investigate the possibility.

Gradually we noticed that our house was too small for the three children and all their friends. Yes, Mark began having neighborhood children come over and play, and Leslie always had frequent visitors. I decided to start a campaign for a new house. With the age levels of our brood, it was impossible to accommodate everyone under the setup that we had. Karleen, our little one, was often woken up by the noise in the house. My husband soon concurred.

I wanted to move into the New Trier High School district because we had heard and read so much about it. We attended an open forum at New Trier West High School one evening and were impressed by the caliber of the school board. We soon noticed however, that all the houses in that district were out of our price range. Then we found one we could afford, but again, it needed a lot of work. The situation was similar to the first home we had purchased. The house was neglected because the couple living there had gotten divorced, only, in this case, a downtown (Chicago) lawyer had bought it and only superficially fixed it up to turn a profit. We ended up buying it, realizing it would take years before the house would be the way we thought a house ought to be. It was spring 1973 when we finally moved in, after we had labored day and night for two weeks. We had ripped out old carpeting, patched up holes in the walls from BB guns, prepared to paint and painted and painted. Finally, we had new carpet installed in some of the rooms, and then came our

Chapter 11 | Chicago 1966-1976

move. We were exhausted. Having an older daughter had been of immense help. She stayed with our toddler and our son while we slaved on the house until three every morning. Leslie was despondent that she had to abandon her high school (Glenbrook South), for New Trier West. I, however, was very pleased since she had associated with some people we had considered highly undesirable, especially a group of seniors. (She was only a freshman.) She had tried extremely hard to gain status in that school, and I worried about peer pressure and the choices she was making. We had numerous arguments on the amount of time she devoted to schoolwork, compared to the amount of time she spent on her social endeavors. I was hoping New Trier would not be a repeat performance. To ease her alienation we let her have her own phone and her own line in her room. We fixed up her room and decorated it especially nicely. Giving Leslie her own telephone line turned out to be a mistake though. After catching her repeatedly having conversations at two or three in the morning, we shut down her line. She was allowed to keep the phone in her room but it had to be connected to the main house line.

In the summer of 1973, we intended to go to Germany. We were planning to go in late July and were making preparations for the trip.

In June, my brother-in-law Lee called from Phoenix and told us he had just received word that Norman, their older brother in Tucumcari, New Mexico, had committed suicide by shooting himself in the head. He had been ill with severe prostate hypertrophy that was affecting his quality of life. Since he was divorced, and had no immediate family, he chose to end his life so he would not become a burden to his brothers. He was sixty years old, and afraid of becoming an invalid. He thought he might end up in a wheelchair with a colostomy bag. He left lots of notes explaining his conduct.

We were totally stunned. Lynn met Lee in Tucumcari for the funeral. In accordance with Norman's stated wishes, they handled everything together.

We were considering canceling the trip to Germany, but decided to go ahead with it, since there was nothing we could do here after everything was taken care of. It was a smooth trip, and probably good for Lynn to get away.

Tishi   REFUGEE • IMMIGRANT • MOTHER

Our son Mark was eight years old and the only one who did not seem to enjoy this trip to Germany. He kept waking up in the night crying again. It really bothered me, I felt for him. He is very sensitive and the strange environment was too much for him. He seemed fine during the day, but apparently was bothered in his subconscious mind. Leslie had a great time with German boys and girls her own age, and our little Karleen was admired by everybody. At almost four years old, our pretty baby had turned into a beautiful little girl with an outgoing and charming personality.

Once we were back home, Leslie was crushed about having to leave a certain German boy behind. The funny thing was, I had dated his father very briefly as a teenager, and now my daughter and the son were staying connected with letters and packages and occasional phone calls.

One day, after she had gone out with a group of girls, Leslie told us she had a met a boy who reminded her of this particular German boy. The young man did actually call and invite her out on a date. She declined, telling him, and us, that even though he looked a bit like Karl-Heinz from Germany, his eyes were vampire eyes, and she was afraid of him. I will say now that she must have had good instincts, but at the time, when she told me how hurt he was, I told her there was a better, less offensive way to turn him down. She had been quite mean in the way she rebuffed him. He called several times until she finally permitted him to come over and introduce himself to us. He came over with his brother. I was quite taken aback. They were both handsome men in their early twenties; what did they want with a 15 year old girl? They were pleasant to talk to but the taller one, John, gave me an uneasy feeling, which I could not pin down. He called her the next day for a date again and she continued to insult him verbally.

He came by the house the following Sunday to see if Leslie was home. She wasn't, and he asked me if he could use the phone. I said yes, and after making his phone call he involved me in conversation. He was pleasant and polite, but obviously trying to butter up the mother. When Leslie came home I told her she should stop being so rude to the fellow. He called her again and asked if maybe they could double date with his brother and a girl that lived next door to them. They lived together

Chapter 11 | Chicago 1966-1976

in the nearby suburb of Kenilworth. I told Leslie she should go on the double date to be polite, and then to forget the guy after that. Since she didn't seem to care for him anyhow, I did not see any danger, and I thought she should make up for hurting his feelings so many times. Then she could just tell him after their date, that she didn't think they had enough in common for it to work out.

So she went out with him and she came home totally converted and happy, saying how much fun she had and how nice he was. Then I became concerned. I did not like this sudden conversion. But I was told he was going to Madison, Wisconsin, to college, in September. One day that summer when I came home from shopping, he was sitting at our kitchen table and Leslie had prepared soup for both of them. They were eating peacefully, talking away, totally unconcerned about my entrance. It was as if I was invisible. He asked her out on another date, and her father and I told her we did not like it, but by then she had caught fire, and we knew if we did not permit it, she would just meet him secretly on the sly. She has a determined streak in her. She and I had arguments in this regard on a number of occasions. The results had been that the boys in question had come over when we were not home. One time we had come home unexpectedly, and another time a neighbor told us. We were caught like between the Devil and the deep blue sea and we reasoned that if we saw what was going on, we could have more control. So she went out with him again. We were waiting for him to leave soon for Madison. Meanwhile he told her he wanted her to be his girlfriend. I told her to get rid of him. He reminded me of my first great love, about which I still have dire memories. I told her not to get involved with this fellow because he was too smooth, too old and too crafty. My words fell on deaf ears. To Leslie, he had suddenly become the shiny white knight. She promised him she would be his girlfriend. She told us he had just turned 22 years old.

He finally left for college, and his younger brother, who already had finished his degree, showed up to take Leslie to a movie. When John heard about it he objected strenuously and the brother refrained from coming over.

Meanwhile our son Mark was having a hard time getting adjusted to the new school. Being shy by nature, he always had trouble making new friends. He was quite upset about being in a new environment, new school, new faces. He did not deal with it well. We were fully aware of it and tried to be understanding, but it was he who finally had to deal with it. His teacher turned out to be a perfectionist who was perturbed that he would not cooperate with her testing methods. She wanted to determine his standing and was becoming frustrated with him. I tried to explain to her that he was suffering from not having his old friends and being in an unfamiliar environment, but she felt that possibly something else might be wrong with him. She wanted him tested by the school psychologist. We consented.

The report from the psychologist was encouraging. She found him deficient in auditory discrimination, which we knew, but she also said that his abstract reasoning power was that of a twelve year old. He was only eight at the time. Apparently he had strong opinions and his own mind, and was not going to accommodate her unless he deemed it proper. He seemed to find the tests uninteresting and unnecessary so she had some trouble testing him also, but she was not disturbed by it. She thought his teacher had overreacted. She did think that Mark's development was inhibited by the female triangle at home: mother, older sister, younger sister. I explained that Mark and his older sister had a good relationship and that she loved him very much. He had some typical sibling rivalry with his younger sister but he really liked them both. The answer was not about their relationships, it was about their existence, particularly having an older sister who was a strong personality. It was the situation of being born between them, not what they may or may not be doing. I did not quite believe it but I can see now that she was right. Since his big sister has been away at college, there is a definite change in his demeanor, personality and performance. It seems like he is becoming his own person.

A couple years before college, Leslie's relationship with John went on our nerves, but we lived with it, hoping it would soon be over. It kept on going by mail and phone calls and visits, up to the summer of 1974. Then John discovered an older girl and said goodbye to Leslie. We felt sorry for her, but told her that this was the right thing for both of them,

Chapter 11 | Chicago 1966-1976

and that he was way too old for her anyhow. At this point she became hysterical, swearing he was the love of her life, and blurting out that he was actually 25! At that point I became hysterical, Lynn became gruff, and Leslie ran out of the house to a friends house, where she stayed the whole weekend. She could not take any more tension at that point.

We found most of our life revolving around her and her heartbreak, and were troubled when, after eight weeks of absence, John made contact with her again. She was naturally happy but wary, and treated him sort of coolish. Here we had thought we were rid of him and there he was again. It was pitting a heavyweight against a lightweight. He was too worldly for her. There was a total imbalance.

Leslie began running to high school parties and on the side, going out with John again. When he left for Wisconsin once more, in the fall of 1974, I went with my husband to Mexico City, to a work-related meeting. I had an older lady stay with the children. When we came back, I noticed a change for the negative in Leslie. She was restless and secretive. We soon found out she had gone out with the brother of John again, and gotten sexually involved with him. I read her diary. I felt I had to, because I knew something was going on and Leslie did not seem like herself. She had written in a sort of code, but it was pretty easy to figure out. I did not confront her with what I knew, instead, I made remarks at her strange behavior. One night she came home with my car and acted sort of strange. Lynn was already asleep. I talked to her, but I could not put my finger on it, it was more intuition than anything else. The next day when I wanted to use my car, I opened the door and stale air like from a bar hit me in the face. It reeked of liquor and cigarettes. I now had reason to confront my daughter, who stonewalled me. I got zero results. She said she had no idea why it smelled like this. I was furious and told her she could not share my car for quite some time.

Meanwhile I heard her talking to two of her girlfriends on the phone. I felt compelled to listen in. She was referring to the outing she had with John's brother and how fantastic sex was by the lake. So I knew she was still seeing him.

John came home for the weekend to see her. She went out with him and later I heard her on the phone with one of her girlfriends (I did a lot of listening in at the time), telling her how great it was to fake an orgasm with John while she was thinking of his brother Dan.

I finally found a note on her bed in her room from one of her friends giving her advice on how to deal with the brother, who was not dropping his own girlfriend, but cheating with Leslie. She was becoming distrustful of him too, and increasingly unhappy, I could tell.

This note gave me something concrete, some definite evidence with which I could address the issue with her. I told her that this was not the way to exact revenge on either of them and that she was messing with a family. She broke down and admitted she wanted to get rid of the brother, and she was done with getting back at John, and disgusted with herself and Dan and the whole thing anyhow.

The next thing she wanted to do was to go see John over the weekend. We decided to let her go, this being better than getting together with the brother again, possibly. She came back all in love with John again.

Things calmed down around our house and in November of 1974, my husband Lynn was offered a position as clinical monitor in the Department of Obstetrics and Gynecology at G.D. Searle, which he accepted, and to which he gladly moved into. Just after he accepted it, but was still in research, his boss, the one he had problems with, got fired. By then he had antagonized the people above him as well as the ones below him and he got what he deserved. Lynn never the less moved over to the clinical department and has been extremely content with his work situation.

The great love of Leslie and John lasted until she became pregnant in the spring of 1975. She was 17 years old. I had been unable to get her see a gynecologist and be fitted for a diaphragm. She insisted they used condoms. The truth was they also used the unreliable rhythm method. John took care of her and the abortion. She paid part of the fee but he carried the main financial burden. I was concerned about her emotional well being, so I acted no differently than if she had some virus, like the flu. I think she appreciated it at the time. The Concord Medical Center assigned her to a woman gynecologist who was extremely unpleasant and judgmental with Leslie, but did get her started with a diaphragm. I was happy about the diaphragm, however Leslie

Chapter 11 | Chicago 1966-1976

did not want to ever go back to that woman again. I assured her we would find a nice doctor for regular check ups, and at this point she agreed, finally listening to reason.

Leslie learned John had been to a girl's house while she had been home recovering from the abortion. She decided that was it, she was going to break up with him, for good. It turned out, there was a cute boy at school with whom she wanted to go out. I was elated that she was interested in someone her own age. He is her present boyfriend. It took awhile, but she shed John for Jim, the cute guy. He asked her out on a date and they went out every so often until it developed into a steady relationship in the summer. That following November she went out on her own with some friends to a party, where she flirted heavily with one of the boys at the party. Jim heard about it and broke off the relationship with her. They conversed once in awhile but did not go out. She was so sad, and this time she had started the mess. She put us through hell. It was impossible to live with her. That was the time she told us she wanted to hitchhike to California and become a cocktail waitress. I wondered what would happen next. Jim's family stepped in and invited Leslie to go out to dinner with them. They felt that their son really liked her and that his behavior was out of proportion to what she had done. So Jim and Leslie made up at Christmas and things took a turn for the better until Easter. We were staining eggs when Leslie told us she was pregnant again. We did not want to believe it, but it was true. We were not as sympathetic as the first time and I told her if it happens again, I don't want to know about it anymore, she would have to handle it herself. After the second abortion she luckily was assigned to a very pleasant male gynecologist whose patient she wants to remain. She seems to have a rapport with him.

Meanwhile Karleen, our little one, turned into a little girl whose voice cannot be ignored. She hears and sees everything and is the policeman in the family, as we call her. She sees to it that nothing is forgotten and thinks ahead to the duties of the next day. She does this for the whole family!

Our son Mark has developed along normal lines. He is less shy, runs around with other boys, forgets his homework at times, but has greatly improved overall with his schoolwork since his eldest sister went off to college.

Getting Leslie to college was a task in itself. One time we only wanted to discuss the possibilities and she ran away and stayed at a friends house. We usually were able to find out where she was without her knowing it.

Getting applications filled out and in on time was another problem. She rebelled against everything, saying all along she did not even know if she wanted to go to college. However, all the jobs she held during summers and after school bored her terribly. College was the only answer. Now she is doing well, but she always has another trick up her sleeve, who knows what the next one will be?

My husband and I hope we learned from our first experience and will apply our knowledge in raising our other two children, who are quite different from our first, and quite different from each other. Again, who knows what's in store for us, but at least we have more experience now.

During this past year I had to stay on medication for my intestines because my digestive track suffered again from all the pressure in our home situation.

Chapter 11 | Chicago 1966-1976

Karleen, 1974

Karleen and Mark, Xmas 1975

Below: Mark, Tishi & Karleen, Colorado, 1977

Lynn, Karleen & Mark, Colorado, 1977

Tishi REFUGEE • IMMIGRANT • MOTHER

Epilogue
2017

...And so ends my mother's recollection of her life. Just like that. Within two and a half years, so would her life. Those digestive issues either caused or were the result of, gallstones developed from poor nutrition in her childhood during and after the war. About a year after writing this, during a routine gallstone removal she finally agreed to, she had a small number of gallbladder cancer cells removed, and was told that what was removed was intact, had not spread, and she needed no further treatment, except for monthly scans. It was a scare, but after twelve months of scans, she was declared cancer free and all clear. My parents celebrated with champagne in January of 1979. In February, she went on a ski trip with my Dad, Mark and Karleen. By April she was feeling off again, but went on a family road trip to Virginia and Kentucky, visiting Thomas Jefferson's home of Monticello. The trip was cut short, as she had severe leg pain, which came from small blood clots caused by a malfunctioning liver, we found out later. My sister Karleen told me how our Mom had her legs up the whole drive home and seemed to be in a lot pain. No one knew how serious it was, but within days of coming home and being admitted to the hospital, one of those blood clots went to her brain, and she went into a brief coma and died. She was 44 years old. I talked to her on the phone from Los Angeles right before she slipped into the coma. She would meander from coherent conversation into nonsensical non sequiturs, yet always insisting she was fine, she was going to be just fine. I was on the next plane to Chicago, but by the time I landed, she was unconscious and her vitals were not good. I was 21, my little sister Karleen was 9, and my little brother Mark was 14. I remember washing Karleen's hair in the shower trying to explain that our mom was not coming home. Karleen could not seem to process this information, asking me question after question until she suddenly got it. We just stood in the shower together crying. Our mom passed away early the next morning.

It was only after the autopsy that we even knew about the blood clots, and what had caused them. The cancer had come back with a vengeance and spread unchecked to her liver. A malfunctioning liver was not cleaning her blood, causing the clots that killed her. It happened so rapidly, it might as well have been a car accident. My sister remembers it differently. She remembers all the years of stomach problems, the bout with cancer, our mom seemingly weaker and more depressed and worried...one time telling my sister she was scared and didn't want to die. My brother Mark, after losing his mom at 14, partially shut down and disconnected. He was present, and he wasn't cold, but he did not want to spend any time discussing it. As the years went by, he seemed to heal in a healthy way, and now is quite open to talking about her and eager to learn more about her heritage. Both my brother and sister are married and have children. I am amicably divorced after a long marriage, and have two incredible grown sons. All our children have our mom's feistiness, and I'm sure she would have been in awe of all her grandchildren.

My dad, after being devastated by the loss of our mom, went on to remarry, and was with our stepmother until his death. He had several health issues in his 80's but ultimately died from pneumonia at 86.

We have a wonderful half sister Kirstin from their marriage.

After our mom's passing, Dad, being a medical researcher, scoured the family on my mother's side for any history of cancer, and found none. He spoke and wrote to her doctors and other experts in related fields and concluded that it was "sporadic", not genetic. He surmised that some combination of malnutrition during the war and postwar years, coupled with the burden of guilt and anger she felt about her origins, resulted in her getting cancer. As a medical professional, he seemed dumbfounded that he had not been able to see it earlier or save her.

Epilogue 2017

I did not go to the funeral in Germany. We had a memorial service in Chicago, at Northwestern University in a tiny chapel my mother loved. A few months later, my sister Karleen and brother Mark went to Germany with our dad, who did a curious thing. Before the service, he took them on a tour of Dachau, one of the horrific concentration camps. My sister never asked him why, but I think he thought our mom would have wanted them to see. He was in such anguish, who can say. But Grossvati, our grandfather, our mom's dad, was extremely displeased with our father for that. He thought it was the last thing grieving children needed to go through. He was also unhappy that our dad was keeping part of our mom's ashes to be spread over Lake Michigan, near her last home. He wanted to know what part of her did he, as her father, have? A leg, an arm? That was how he put it. He pulled my sister aside and told her that yes, it was terrible to lose a parent, especially at such a young age.

"But", he added, in broken English, losing his composure, "your own child is not supposed to die before you." Like my father, and the rest of the family, he was devastated. His heart was not to be mended, it seemed. He died five years later of heart failure in his sleep.

Tishi REFUGEE • IMMIGRANT • MOTHER

Addendum

A Daughter's Reaction and Recollections

PART 1 – REACTION

The most compelling aspect of reading my mom's story, was the witnessing of repetitive patterns, and noticing that the person re-living the patterns is unaware of them. These patterns did not just emerge in my mom's life, but I recognized familial patterns, stretching from my grandmother down to my own children. When my mother began to write her life down on paper, she was 41 or 42, yet she did not seem to draw any correlation between her relationship with her mother, and her relationship with me. She mentions how her mother worked hard and saved money so that she, her daughter, could attend the higher levels of the educational system. Her mother sacrificed for her, yet even at 42, my mom merely acknowledges that fact, without much sign of any gratitude. This could partially be attributed to her objective writing style, yet I do recognize the same characteristics in myself. It took me a long time to comprehend all my parents did for me.

I recognized parts of the mom I knew, but there was also the discovery of someone I didn't know, someone who was a lot more like me, both as a child and an adult.

It is clear that she experienced her mother as smothering and controlling. When Grossmutti (our grandmother, her mom) worried about her working in Geneva, or didn't want her to go to school in Munich, my mom found her mom's concern overreaching. When my mom married my dad and was about to move to America, it seemed as though she wanted to just break free from her own mother's suctioning tentacles.

Tishi   REFUGEE • IMMIGRANT • MOTHER

To wit, many years later, I found Mommy to be obsessive about me, reading my journals, listening to my phone calls, and the constant questions regarding my boyfriends. She acted as if I was on drugs, or in trouble with the law, when I was just being a teenager and dating, albeit with high drama and two abortions.

My mom's aim always, was to be candid with me, and I knew she had sex before she met my father. I always thought she was so cool for being straight with me. In the 70's there were still a lot of parents who had not had sex before marriage, or certainly were not open about it if they had. So, as much as my mom told me she thought it was a healthy thing to have some experience, and something to compare to before you settle down with someone for the rest of your life, she was only candid to the point of her own comfort. That comfort line was a little farther out than most parents, but, I came to find, not as far out as the truth. I was told she had been with only one man before our father. Given my proclivities in my teen years, when she was discussing this with me, I can understand her judgment call of not exposing her entire roster of sexual encounters. I was dating older men, and I can see how that would cause concern, but that is exactly what she had been doing as a teenager. My most alarming transgressions were having the two abortions, something my father, who specialized in research on birth control, found particularly humiliating. As it turned out, two abortions were exactly what my mother had unsuccessfully sought out for herself. It was a shock to discover that my sister and I almost did not exist. I do remember Mommy calling Karleen "the best mistake I ever made", but I had no idea she had actually attempted to terminate that pregnancy. Carina and Mark were the only planned children. I still believe philosophically in a woman's right to choose, and I would have to defer to fate, destiny, or divine providence to explain why that new information only gave me momentary pause.

As the child of a biologist, I have an educated opinion regarding consciousness versus multiplying cells. I am pro-choice, but only up to ten weeks into the pregnancy, and after that, only if there is direct danger to the mother's life, or a grave problem with the fetus.

Clearly, it was an epic experience for me to unearth such pertinent

Addendum | A Daughter's Reaction and Recollections

personal information. I do not feel deceived by any of my discoveries. I trust, accept, and can understand the reasoning.

Further revelations include the story about Grossvati being captured and held in an American prisoner-of-war camp. I had always been told that it was the Russians who got him. There are no older living relatives to explain this discrepancy, although I suspect that my grandfather finally wanted to freely share his stories about the hardships he underwent, like having to eat grass and dirt to survive. Since my dad was American, he didn't want me to feel he, or the family, had any hostility towards us.

I was also told it was my great uncle who was in politics, not my great-grandfather. He was the one who joined the Nazi party at one point, and as Mayor, greeted Hitler personally. I heard plenty about this "great uncle", who really did not like Hitler, and was disliked by the Nazi's for not acting "German enough". I knew that he was big in post-war German government and part of the rebuilding of Germany. I was never told that he met Hitler.

In researching and fact checking for this project, the discovery of the German Expulsion after the war really sunk in for me. I remember visiting a castle several times, as do my brother and sister. We always went to one large room, and our mom stood in an alcove corner and said she lived in that spot for half a year as a refugee, with her mother and sister. I don't think we really understood what that meant. We always took photos in that corner and around the castle. I have a hazy memory of being told how and why she had lived there, but it was so outside my sense of reality that I could not comprehend it. Karleen, Mark and I just thought of it as that war stuff she went through.

There is also the possibility that it was only vaguely explained or described to us. My sister Karleen thinks that maybe our mom didn't want to burden her kids with that kind of weighty information. The cleansing of ethnic Germans after the war and blaming them of collective guilt, are taboo subjects that no side wants to revisit. The Czechs, the Germans and the Allies all have their reasons for discouraging discussion of that event. I am grateful that my mother and her family were not among its casualties.

On a happier note, my research did lead me to discover that I am a descendant of a people who dwelled in the Bohemian forest. Personally, this rounds out my identity in a way that makes sense for me.

Karleen and I often wonder how Mommy would have reacted to today's world. I had her until I was 21, my sister was only 9 when she died. I have always tried to fill in the blanks for Karleen. She feels so lucky to have a way now, to know her mother more. Whereas I have strong memories of Mommy's political rants, Karleen, who is involved in politics herself, now can form her own ideas regarding our mom's personal political views. It is apparent from her writing that our mom was quite left leaning, and considered herself liberal. She supported Democrats, but shied away from identifying as one. She was the first person I knew to call themselves an Independent.

I recall Mommy being wary of Nationalism of any kind. It was ingrained in Germans of her generation never to put country "above all else", as was Hitler's motto. I have no doubt that Trump's "America First" slogan would have made her shudder. She loved the United States and celebrated Independence Day on July 4th, but too much flag waving made her nervous. She was not one for group-think, or mob mentality. She cautioned me to always think for myself, and no matter how many people are doing something or raving about it, if it doesn't feel right to me, I should pause and analyze, keeping an open mind. If it still doesn't sit well with me, I should never let anyone dictate what my actions or ideology should be if my personal logic cannot reconcile with it. Nor should I ever fear expressing my opinion, as long as it is thought through and I can back it up with facts.

The person she presented to me as my mother, is the same person that emerged from her pages. I now have a deeper understanding of who that person was and why, which also gives me priceless insight about who I am.

Addendum | A Daughter's Reaction and Recollections

PART 2 – RECOLLECTIONS

When I was a baby, a toddler, and a small child, we watched fireworks from a distance because, as parents know, they can be frightening for children. In 1965, when my dad had a research position at Cornell University in Ithaca, New York, I was seven years old and excited and ready to see fireworks up close for the first time. My dad had gotten us coveted seats inside the stadium at Cornell. I loved it. I was in awe. I noticed my mom squirming and covering her ears, and I turned to laugh with her, when I realized she wasn't having fun. Right then, the kind of fireworks that are just loud blasts, and look like white bullet holes in a dark sky, went off. Mommy was holding her head and shaking it back and forth, saying "NOoo!" She started to cry, clutching one of our blankets to cover her ears. Then she jumped up and ran out of the stadium. My dad grabbed me and we caught up to her. She was angry at him for not realizing how loud and close this was, and how it looked and sounded like one of the worst nights of her life. We never brought her to see fireworks again. She stayed home, with the cat, "like a cat", she would joke. Until I read about her life, I never fully comprehended why she couldn't just enjoy them.

Mommy's upbringing during World War II and the aftermath colored her whole life, and seemed to more so, as she got older. From my pre-teen years into my teens, she carried that German guilt heavily on her shoulders. She dragged me to every movie that addressed it: "The Garden of the Finzi-Contini's", to Maximillian Schell's "The Man In the Glass Booth", to "Cabaret". She died before "The Holocaust" aired on television, followed by the subsequent proliferation of Holocaust themed films. I have seen them all as well, from "Sophie's Choice" to "Schindler's List", to "Inglourious Bastards", as well as many smaller independents. Most recently I saw "The Zookeeper's Wife". They are all excellent films, but I cringe to think of the pain they would have caused my mom. I hope she would have come to a place of peace about the subject. She was proud of so many facets of being German. We celebrated Christmas the German way, on Christmas Eve, with German Christmas

Tishi   REFUGEE • IMMIGRANT • MOTHER

carols. She raised me to speak, read and write in German. This was a more difficult task the more American she became, so my siblings did not benefit as I did, from her being, basically, fresh off the boat, even though it was a plane. But the longer she was in America, the more guilty and conflicted she became, possibly because we ultimately moved to an area that was more Jewish than any we had lived in before. Mommy did begin to wear a delicate silver necklace with a silver pendant in the shape of a little mezuzah, to show her solidarity with our neighbors.

When I was in third grade in Northbrook, Illinois, I made a menorah out of tin foil and stuck little birthday candles in it. Our neighborhood was predominantly Jewish, and most of my friends were celebrating Chanukah at the time. I placed my homemade menorah in our front window, under our Christmas lights, and I was quite pleased with myself. I thought it made me fit in with my friends at school. I called my mom into the living room to light the candles for me, and she was horrified. She swiped it up and tried to explain to me that she was German and everyone in the neighborhood knew that. She said a tinfoil menorah with birthday candles under our Christmas lights would look like she was being disrespectful. I remember crying because I didn't understand at all. She attempted to educate me about World War II, in a way she thought a third grader could handle. She explained that after the War, in German schools, they didn't know how to teach that part of history, so for her generation, it was just sort of skimmed over and basically skipped. It wasn't until she came to the United States that she realized to the full extent, what happened to the Jews. She told me that in the following generations they beat it into German kids heads, and the new generations of Germans share a collective shame. She didn't think that was necessarily so good either. The whole issue tormented her.

My childhood was definitely experienced through a different lens than many of my friends. As a grown-up, I have come to find that most people feel that way about their own childhoods for one reason or another. My reason obviously, was having a mother from a different country with different traditions, food, folklore, history, and most obviously, a different language.

On the food front, imagine the reactions of my fellow third graders

Addendum | A Daughter's Reaction and Recollections

when I opened up my "Casper the Friendly Ghost" lunch box in the cafeteria, and the smell of packed up liverwurst and sauerkraut wafted their way. It took a few sessions of me arguing with my mom to the point of bursting into tears, until she finally relented and let me take baloney sandwiches and Fritos, like everyone else. She insisted it wasn't as healthy or fresh, but I promised to eat all her food for dinner every night. The thing was, Mommy cooked her sauerkraut in beer and milk, with garlic, butter and sugar. It was not what people think of when they think of sauerkraut. It was actually quite tasty. But it still stank to high heaven after a morning in Tupperware.

I had made my mom so happy with my ability to speak her mother tongue. Then, to her dismay, around 9 or 10, I began denying and rejecting German. If we were out clothes shopping for instance, she would speak to me in German. This was also a way to openly discuss prices and quality without seeming rude. However, these conversations drew quizzical looks from other shoppers, and it began to bother me. It was not as diverse a country back then, and certainly not in the Midwest, in Glenview, Illinois. I refused to answer my mother in German. I understood everything she said, but I responded only in English, leaving my mother to feel like an actor on an improv stage whose fellow improv scene partner denies something the one actor has already stated. It's the number one no-no in improv etiquette. One never just leaves their fellow actor hanging in the wind. And that is essentially what I did. My mom's manner of handling it was to stubbornly continue speaking in German, and I, just as stubbornly, continued to respond in English, which also exposed her opinions of the merchandise. We would bicker about it on the way home, and I would tell her that people looked at us strangely, to which she would retort, "Well, they must be strange then!", eliciting an exasperated, patronizing eye-roll from me.

As much as my mom admired the relaxed American way of life, she never shook off a certain European formality. Although we were not church people, Sundays were family days, and if we went out anywhere on a Sunday, we had to dress up. If we went to anyone's house for dinner, we had to dress up. If we flew on an airplane, we had to dress up. Granted, in the 60's, everyone dressed for occasions more than they did in the 70's and later. But people did wear jeans to eat at a casual place like Howard Johnson's. Not our family. Even going to the zoo, I had to wear dresses, my brother and dad were in suits, and my mom also wore sleek, elegant dresses and pumps.

Enter Mrs. Warner, my fantasy mom. She lived across the street and was friends with my mother. Her son Stevie was right between my brother's age and mine, so he played with both of us. Mrs. Warner was tall, blue eyed and had strawberry blonde hair like the comic strip character Brenda Starr. She always wore pink lipstick and colorful, fluffy, but tight fitting dresses over her curves. She had the sweetest voice with just a hint of a Southern drawl. I was tall for my age, greenish-blue eyed and blonde. I even had a hint of strawberry color in my hair (I hoped), and I believed that Joanie Warner looked and sounded more like what someone who was my mother should look and sound like. I thought she resembled a Barbie doll or a movie star. Mr. Warner, Joanie's husband, had taught my mom to drive. He was the PE instructor, driver's ed teacher, and swim coach at a nearby high school, Niles West. My parents had not gotten far with driving lessons on their own. My father said it was a known fact that driving instruction and marriage were a bad mix. But the driving lessons with Mr. Warner were a success. So Joanie and my mom both drove, and on extremely cold or rainy or snowy days, they traded off picking us up from school. We usually walked home, but on the days that ruffly Joanie showed up, I was excited and proud. Around ten years of age, kids normally begin to be hyper-critical of their parents. I found my mother's politics, accent, and opinions annoying. Her sense of style in clothes and haircuts was European and high fashion influenced, which I found jarring . I just wanted a brownie baking American mother, who would let me wear my cords to a restaurant. So when people at school saw Mrs. Warner coming for me, whether she walked into the school or just pulled up in her car, I acted like she was my mom. At school performances, she would sit near my mom and wave at her son, and I would wave back. My mom would think I was waving at her, and the kids I didn't know that well, weren't certain who my mom was. I allowed them to be confused. It gave me a secret pleasure with a dash of guilt.

Addendum | A Daughter's Reaction and Recollections

Mom had her own internal conflicts. She grew frustrated with so many things American, as she struggled to raise children the only way she knew how. As enamored as she was with America's easy life and the space and room to breathe, she was disappointed and taken aback by some of the social mores in the U.S. On the one hand, she had these severe standards of protocol regarding attire and manners, where Americans were more laid back; but on the other, she subscribed to the relaxed European mentality when it came to sexuality and the human body. I remember going swimming at lakes and insisting she take me to a changing room for fear of someone seeing my private parts. She would tell me to change under the towel and that no one had any interest in my genitalia. Just the use of that word sent me into fits, and she would worry that I thought of any part of my body as naughty or dirty or embarrassing. I would then tell her that what I found most embarrassing was her.

One summer afternoon in 1968 we were at Flick Pool in Glenview. I was ten years old, my brother Mark was three. He was an adorably cute toddler. Flick was a public pool in the nice suburb of Chicago where we lived. I thought it was great, but I had not yet been to a German public pool. After I experienced one, I could understand why Mommy complained about the fences between the snack and pool area and that there was too much concrete and no grassy area to picnic on. In Germany, going to the pool is almost like going to a lake. There are rolling green lawns, several pools of varying depth and size, all with mini-moats and little foot showers so no grass gets in the pools. They had giant water slides at regular public pools long before we had water parks here. The German mindset is clean and litter aware, so no one leaves food particles or candy wrappers lying around, as we witnessed at Flick. I thought my mom made too big a deal out of it, but again, having been to German pools now, I do get it. In Germany, little kids run around naked and little girls under about ten just wear bathing suit bottoms. As we settled in, my mother undressed my little brother and let him run free. She didn't have much experience with the contained area of American pools, since we frequented lakes in parks with beaches usually. We were by the kiddie pool, and Mark was daytime potty-trained, so my mom

Tishi   REFUGEE • IMMIGRANT • MOTHER

was contentedly watching him splash around, when she was startled out of her dream state by a loud whistle, aimed at her. A young lifeguard came up to her shouting, "What do you think you are doing ma'am?" He was pointing at my nude little brother Mark frolicking with other toddlers, all blissfully unaware of their clothing or lack thereof. My mother's mouth dropped open in surprise.

"What do you mean?!" she practically spat back at him in her clearly accented voice.

"Well, I don't care what they do where you come from, but here we cover up children. That is indecent exposure," the lifeguard responded. Mommy called him indecent. I started to wander off to the big pool, once again, feeling mortified by my foreign mom. The lifeguard added, "Cover that child up or you will have to leave the pool," then shook his head, muttering under his breath, "What is wrong with you?" I stopped and turned to my mom, urging her to just comply, but she was on the warpath. She brushed past me in her navy two-piece with white piping and went right up to the lifeguard, pointing her finger at his face. "What is wrong with YOU?", she said loudly, "It's a little boy, what in the HELL is wrong with you?". She grabbed me, my brother, and all our stuff and we left the pool.

She did not love that part of America at all. She found it uptight and puritanical. She had no tolerance for that type of repression.

I, on the other hand, just wanted to be American. Later that summer of 1968, we traveled to Germany to see our relatives. Riding around in Grossvati's Mercedes, I enlisted my brother Mark to help me hold up two signs I made for the back window. I had used watercolors to paint American flags on white shirt cardboards and wrote WE ARE USA and ALL THE WAY!, in magic marker. Every time we passed a tank or transport truck of American GI's, we held the signs up, eliciting whistles, honks and claps from the servicemen as we drove by. The grown-ups in the front seat, whether it was my grandfather, uncle, aunt or parents, kept wondering why that kept happening. They were so involved in their own conversations, they didn't bother to investigate, but Mark and I would just pull down the signs and hide them, holding in our laughter. I think I was trying to assert or find my own identity, not meaning any-

Addendum | A Daughter's Reaction and Recollections

thing against my mom or Germany. Mark was just giggly about being complicit in mischief with his big sister.

In May of 1969, my parents threw me a spring party. I had about ten girlfriends over for the afternoon. We played badminton and volleyball in our backyard, climbed our apple tree, and then sat at the picnic table and were waited on by my mom and dad. Dad barbecued burgers and hot dogs, and my mom served us her delicious German potato salad. We were drinking Dad's Root Beer, and were probably on a pre-teen sugar high. We got boisterous and silly, and somehow the party exploded into a food fight. My mother was appalled. She basically lost it. She gave us a verbal dressing down about wasting food when there are people scrounging for one morsel of what we were whipping at each other. She told us she knew this because she had to scrounge for meals when she had been our age. She called us ungrateful affluent brats and stomped off, saying we could clean up our own mess. I wanted to sink into my chair and on into the patio and let it swallow me up. The silence and gaping mouths on my friends faces were humiliating, and portended whispers around school for weeks to come.

My dad saved the day with ice cream bars for dessert and some goofy jokes. Somehow, with his joking around, he smoothed things over to the point where we were all running through the sprinklers later and laughing. Everyone went home happy, and with goody bags that my mom showed up to hand out. She gave a quick apology for overreacting, and at school everyone talked about the great party and the food fight that made Leslie's mom mad, but was really fun. I could live with that, and I was grateful to my dad for diffusing the situation.

The worst example of the disconnect I had regarding my mom not being American-born occurred when I was 13 years old. I don't recall if I was having a hormonal mood swing due to my period, but it is certainly a possibility. I just know I was feeling fed up with being called a Kraut and a Nazi. A new little kid in the neighborhood rang our doorbell, asking if my little brother Mark could come out and play. My mom told him that Mark was busy, but would come out in a little while. I think she was doing speech exercises with him at the time. I went out a little later to walk over to a friend's house. The new little kid was hanging

Tishi   REFUGEE • IMMIGRANT • MOTHER

around waiting for my brother. "Hey," he yelled, "how come your mom talks funny?" Without batting an eyelash, I tossed these words back over my shoulder: "That's not our mom, that's the cleaning lady." As the steam of those words literally hung in the cold air, I walked on, always feeling like I was a traitor in that moment. Funny thing was, the kid was really young, like maybe six years old. He didn't come around often, and since my brother wasn't that social, that kid only saw my mom once in awhile. I never said anything to him or my brother about it. I do wonder if he always thought she was our cleaning lady?

As a teen-ager, there was an aspect of my mom's German background that served as a benefit, and that was her attitude towards alcohol. She didn't understand American laws that stated 18 year old boys could be sent to war, but were not allowed to have a beer. In Europe, drinking ages are implied, but not strictly enforced. In Germany the legal age to drink beer and wine is 16. For spirits the age is 18. Older children drinking a little wine with their family at dinner is an accepted part of European culture.

In February of 1973, I was going to a dance at Glenbrook South High School in Glenview. My date Nicky came to pick me up with his friend Dan and Dan's girlfriend, my friend Christy. We took all the requisite photos, and then, as we got into the car to head to the dance, my mom ran out of the house with a bottle of champagne and four plastic cups, saying "This is for you all to share. Don't open it until you are at the dance, and drink it early, so you can drive later...and have fun!" You can imagine the looks on my friends faces as we drove off, after thanking her. They started whooping and yelling how super cool Leslie's mom was. I felt special. The night went sour though, when we tried to open the bottle in the snowy parking lot. The car was too cramped, but it was freezing outside, and none of us were well versed in opening champagne. It took a long time and a lot of effort to finally pop the cork. We were trying to keep the noise level down, but we attracted campus security and were 'busted'. I wouldn't describe it as a negative experience, because it turned us into mini-celebrities for a few days. The parents of my friends involved were all level headed and didn't express anger towards my parents. Everyone was called to the school office, and my outspoken

Addendum | A Daughter's Reaction and Recollections

mother kept going on about how four people were not going to get drunk on one bottle of champagne, nor would driving be impaired with that amount of alcohol after a two and a half hour dance. She didn't get the point that in this country, minors are not supposed to ingest alcohol under the age of 21, period. This was her first experience with the fact that in America, the drinking age is enforced, not implied. My dad stepped in and explained the situation in his disarmingly soft-spoken manner. The students involved were suspended from school for three days. Yes, seriously, we just didn't have to go to school. Of course we had to make up the work we missed, but the point was, we didn't have to go to school! We were only underclassmen as freshman and sophomores, so it also did not go on the dreaded "permanent record". And everyone thought my mom was the best.

During my teenage years, Mommy thought that my friends and I had idiotic conversations. She couldn't understand why we didn't sit around having coffee and talking politics. At 13, 14, 15, I thought she was nuts. All I cared about was boys, beer, soda pop, alcohol and rock music. Of course that was in the 1970's, when Starbucks didn't exist and teens never thought to drink coffee except to stay up cramming for exams. She regarded us American kids as unaware and out of touch, living with an unrealistic sense of security, so sure that nothing could ever happen to us. She said that it was a luxury we enjoyed but that we needed to keep ourselves informed. She perceived us as just filling our heads with the next best thing we would throw out later that year. She speculated that if my friends and I cared more about what was going on in the rest of the world, including the world of the arts, that our lives would be richer. She took it upon herself to enrich mine, and I am forever grateful for all the works of human skill and imagination I was exposed to. At the time I was resistant, always worried about missing out on a party. I am so lucky she dragged me to the Kingston Mines, a blues club in downtown Chicago, where I got to watch legends like Lefty Dizz and Magic Slim. We also went to Second City on a regular basis, and an experimental theater called The Body Politic, where on more than one occasion I saw nude actors onstage, at which I would giggle, until a stern look from my mom would set me straight. My dad was always game for taking in a play or seeing music. We went to the Goodman Theater, The Ballet Folklorico, we saw Baryshnikov, the opera Carmen and we made countless trips to the Art Institute of Chicago. On occasion I would bring a friend, and those are wonderful memories. There is a picturesque outdoor amphitheater called Ravinia in the suburbs near where we lived. As a teen I went to rock concerts there with my friends. But from sixth to eighth grade, my mom took me to see symphonies there. Although Mommy called herself modern, she didn't go in for pop music much, except for the Beatles. She loved her classical music, especially Bach, Mozart and Beethoven. Her favorite conductor was Leonard Bernstein, and we always got tickets when he came to town.

On Sunday mornings we slept late and then Mommy made brunch. We either listened to classical music, Herb Alpert, the soundtrack to Zorba the Greek, or her favorite album of Mexican music. For that one, she donned a sombrero and danced around the living room. Two of her other favorites were "Eine Kleine Nachtmusik"(A Little Night Music) and "The Moldau", by Bedrich Smetana. I only recently learned that "The Moldau" was the German name given to the Vltava river, and the music was about the course of its current. That river runs through Czechoslovakia, so I can only assume that the vigor with which she waltzed around and hummed to that piece, came from wonderful memories deep in the best part of her childhood before the war.

Being our mom was her greatest passion, at least from what I saw of her short life. And for all my hang ups about her, I loved her deeply. I always called her Mommy, except for an era as a teenager, when I called her Mother(more like muh-THER, complete with eye-roll). My siblings and I still refer to our parents as Mommy and Daddy. We were just one of those "Mommy and Daddy" families.

Mommy loved our father, and they were fortunate to have the genuine romance that marriage is meant for. Had she lived longer however, I don't believe she would have continued to stand by her man and become a sweet little grandmother. She impressed upon me that a woman should keep her own independent interests alive, and have her own personal goals. As she had been motivated to frequent the lecture circuits at universities, once we settled in on Chicago's North Shore, she regularly

Addendum | A Daughter's Reaction and Recollections

attended seminars at the Chicago Council on Foreign Relations. Her dream was to move to New York after all three kids had flown the nest, and become an interpreter at the United Nations. Her plan was to later retire with our dad to New Mexico and spend their golden years going on archaeological digs searching for ancient relics from the Pueblos. Of course, this was her plan before she discovered Southern California, which she fell in love with. Who knows what direction she would have taken. I am confident she would have actively pursued her interests, and I assume with our Dad by her side.

Mommy was right about me, I did have some "tricks up my sleeve", as she put it. I actually did move out to California and even became a cocktail waitress for a time, just as I had threatened. My parents came out to visit when I was working at the Roxy on Sunset in 1978. Mommy appreciated that I was working around music, and that I was seeing live jazz and blues as well as classic rock. It was not the nightmare my parents had anticipated, in fact, they were both enamored with Southern California. Mommy just gushed about the way everything bloomed year round, and she could not get over the bougainvillea. She became excited about the area, in fact, my dad was making plans to take a position in Irvine, California, when she died.

I developed an acting career, comprised mostly of commercials, some print modeling, and small parts on television shows and in B movies. My mom used to call it a pipe dream, yet confessed to me that she herself, had a secret desire to act at one point. She even had one of her cousins take movie star photo shots of her. I imagine she would've supported me for following my dream.

That dream led to me meeting my husband at a party for one of the films I worked on. We later moved to Sun Valley, Idaho for 14 years to raise our kids away from the city. I wish my mom could have visited us there. She loved to ski, and the mountains would have reminded her of Germany. My two boys are unique, amazing and handsome individuals, as are all the grandchildren. Besides my brother Mark and his family, we all currently reside in California.

Mommy was also right about my sister Karleen. She can still seem like the policewoman of our family. She still has strong opinions about how things should be, and is not shy about sharing them. She inherited Mommy's European formality, and dresses up her kids for events and occasions like our mom did with us. After suffering a hemorrhage and subsequent hysterectomy after childbirth, she is now an advocate for maternal rights for the Unexpected Project. She is also co-founder of We Are Mothergood.

Before she married, Karleen attended college in Chicago. She wrote and starred in a number of plays during her college years, later becoming a spokesmodel for Audi, the German car company. She also worked in public relations and wrote for various Los Angeles magazines throughout the years.

Karleen married a Jewish man named Andrew and converted. They only live a few minutes away from me. On Christmas Eve we all get together and there is a lot of blue under our tree with the Chanukah theme mixed in. Things have come a long way since my tinfoil menorah. No one feels disrespected, and we sing "Dreidel Dreidel Dreidel" as well as "Stille Nacht" (Silent Night in German). My sister has three children: a handsome son and two stunning twin girls, one of whom looks exactly like our mother as a child.

My brother Mark, Mommy's "little fellow", whom she stressed about scholastically, graduated college with a business degree from Western Illinois University. He has a managerial position at Home Depot, and plans to write a science fiction novel. After one divorce, he married Robin, the love of his life, and chose to stay in the Midwest, outside Chicago. He has a gorgeous daughter from his first marriage, and two beautiful stepdaughters with beautiful baby daughters each, from Robin. His daughter came out as gay in her teens and it rocked my brother's world. He has since accepted and embraced her status, and they have a wonderful relationship. Mommy would have championed her granddaughter's individuality, and she would have been very proud of Mark as a father.

A few days before my 21st birthday, my boyfriend Jim had a tragic motorcycle accident and was killed. I came home from LA for the funeral. The morning after, Mommy came into my room, sat down on my bed, and apologized for any mistakes she had made while raising

Addendum | A Daughter's Reaction and Recollections

me. She said I was her first, and she was still learning. She wanted to acknowledge that she had grounded me for too long and too often as punishment for not doing chores, having boys over, or other infractions. I loved her so much for admitting that because I had hated being grounded. I am a social being, and that was like cutting off my lifesblood. She also acknowledged that it had been ineffective, because it only enraged me, and in the long run did not produce positive results. It was so refreshing and validating to hear, and I admire my mother for having that discussion with me. She was gone a few months later, but that conversation has always stayed with me and brought me peace and guidance in dealing with my own children.

Tishi REFUGEE • IMMIGRANT • MOTHER

Clockwise from top: Lincoln Park Zoo all dressed up on a Sunday. Mark doing his "little man" look, 1966; The food fight. I (Leslie) am at the head of the table, ducking to avoid flying food!; Vacation in Green Lake, Wisconsin, Mommy in her navy two-piece with white piping, Summer 1967; Me at 15, with my mom and her sister Inge, Germany, 1973; One of her "movie star" poses; Playing in the waves with me near Point Dume in Malibu, 1978

In Conclusion

My mom loved Jackie Kennedy Onassis and Gloria Steinem and Jane Fonda, and once stated that if there was ever a man she would be with besides my dad, it would be Eugene McCarthy. He ran for president in 1968, but lost the Democratic nomination to Hubert Humphrey, who lost the general election to Richard Nixon. Her second and third choices for love interests were Anthony Quinn and Gregory Peck.

She was fascinated by the book "Bury My Heart at Wounded Knee" because it explores the subject of expansionism, something the Germans were known for. It also reveals much about America, her beloved and adopted home. She was well aware of our history of slavery, but the native American story was not something she had heard much about growing up in Germany. It was the subject that was skimmed over in U.S. public education, at least during my school years.

My mom had strong feelings about the inherent guilt of her childhood religion of Catholicism. She chose to raise us with the Christian values and traditions she viewed as good, right and familiar, minus the dogma. She called herself religious, but not in an organized way. This was in a time before the word spirituality came into vogue. She identified the most with Zen Buddhism, but told us to keep our minds and hearts open. She encouraged us to explore different religions and views, and promised to try to respect whatever choices we made.

Tishi Hunt, nee Anneliese Tichi, was a forthright, progressive force of nature, ahead of her time. She was a stylish and vivacious woman and mom. She passed on many strengths to me and my siblings. Born into privilege, losing everything of material value and social standing, but coming out of it with an intact family, I see her life as blessed. By the luck of the draw she wound up in the democracy of West Germany after the war, and could lead a life where she was free. I see my life as blessed because I had her as my mother. Her foundation had been shaken, but that foundation provided her with a strong sense of self. Although she endured much in her 44 years on planet Earth, she also lived out her dreams. She had moments of sadness, and triggers that set her off, but if you met her, there was no evidence of her history. Although she carried the weight of the horrors she had witnessed, and the deep shame of the ones she had not, her spirit was vibrant with love, and enthusiastic about life. It was an enormous blow to our family to lose her, and a loss to the world, that she is no longer here.

She would have been in her early 80's now.

I froze her in time at around forty years old. I see her dancing around our living room, the stereo blasting the "Mexican Hat Dance" on a Sunday morning, and Mommy alternately wearing and waving a sombrero, and laughing.

In Conclusion

...And the beat goes on...

Tishi   REFUGEE • IMMIGRANT • MOTHER

Kirstin, Karleen and Leslie 2013

Karleen and her family with Susan & Lynn, 2013

Karleen's children at a relative's 2016 wedding

Mark and his wife Robin today

My family 2016, with my two sons and ex-husband

Mark and his lovely daughter

In Conclusion

For more information regarding the German Expulsion, one can do a search for "A Brutal Peace", by Tara Zahra.

For further information on the Sudetenland Germans, as well as maps that show Czechoslovakia's relation to Austria and Germany, see Wikepedia, "Sudetenland Germans" and "German annexation of the Sudetenland". Once you reference one of the maps, it is clear what a circuitous route my mother and her family were taken on, as the train picked up more and more Germans during their nightmare week going from Misslitz to Kulmbach.

Peace

www.ingramcontent.com/pod-product-compliance
Lightning Source LLC
Chambersburg PA
CBHW070054120526
44588CB00033B/1431